PREPARING FOR PRACTICE

Aspen Coursebook Series

PREPARING FOR PRACTICE

Legal Analysis and Writing in Law School's First Year

Set B Case files

AMY VORENBERG
University of New Hampshire School of Law

 Wolters Kluwer

Published by Wolters Kluwer Law in New York.

Wolters Kluwer serves customers worldwide with CCH, Aspen Publishers, and Kluwer Law International products. (www.wolterskluwerlb.com)

To contact Customer Service, e-mail customer.service@wolterskluwer.com, call 1-800-234-1660, fax 1-800-901-9075, or mail correspondence to:

Wolters Kluwer Law & Business
Attn: Order Department
PO Box 990
Frederick, MD 21705

Design and composition by Keithley & Associates, Inc.

Printed in the United States of America.

1 2 3 4 5 6 7 8 9 0

ISBN 978-1-4548-5898-0

Library of Congress Cataloging-in-Publication Data

Vorenberg, Amy, author.
  [Preparing for practice (Set B case files)]
  Preparing for practice : legal analysis and writing in law school's first year : set B case files / Amy Vorenberg, University of New Hampshire School of Law.
    pages cm
  Includes bibliographical references and index.
  ISBN 978-1-4548-5898-0 (alk. paper)
1. Legal composition. 2. Legal research—United States. 3. Practice of law—United States. I. Title.
  KF250.V674 2015
  808.06'634—dc23
                                                          2015033023

About Wolters Kluwer Law & Business

Wolters Kluwer Law & Business is a leading global provider of intelligent information and digital solutions for legal and business professionals in key specialty areas, and respected educational resources for professors and law students. Wolters Kluwer Law & Business connects legal and business professionals as well as those in the education market with timely, specialized authoritative content and information-enabled solutions to support success through productivity, accuracy and mobility.

Serving customers worldwide, Wolters Kluwer Law & Business products include those under the Aspen Publishers, CCH, Kluwer Law International, Loislaw, Best Case, ftwilliam.com and MediRegs family of products.

CCH products have been a trusted resource since 1913, and are highly regarded resources for legal, securities, antitrust and trade regulation, government contracting, banking, pension, payroll, employment and labor, and healthcare reimbursement and compliance professionals.

Aspen Publishers products provide essential information to attorneys, business professionals and law students. Written by preeminent authorities, the product line offers analytical and practical information in a range of specialty practice areas from securities law and intellectual property to mergers and acquisitions and pension/benefits. Aspen's trusted legal education resources provide professors and students with high-quality, up-to-date, and effective resources for successful instruction and study in all areas of the law.

Kluwer Law International products provide the global business community with reliable international legal information in English. Legal practitioners, corporate counsel and business executives around the world rely on Kluwer Law journals, looseleafs, books, and electronic products for comprehensive information in many areas of international legal practice.

ftwilliam.com offers employee benefits professionals the highest quality plan documents (retirement, welfare and non-qualified) and government forms (5500/PBGC, 1099 and IRS) software at highly competitive prices.

MediRegs products provide integrated health care compliance content and software solutions for professionals in healthcare, higher education and life sciences, including professionals in accounting, law and consulting.

Wolters Kluwer Law & Business, a division of Wolters Kluwer, is headquartered in New York. Wolters Kluwer is a market-leading global information services company focused on professionals.

This book is dedicated to my students—
past, present, and future.

About the Author

Professor Amy Vorenberg has been teaching Legal Writing for over 16 years and is currently the Director of Legal Writing at the University of New Hampshire School of Law. She has published numerous articles in the field and presented frequently at academic conferences. She is a current board member of the Association of Legal Writing Directors.

Prior to her academic career, Ms. Vorenberg spent a decade in practice as an Assistant District Attorney in Manhattan, Assistant Attorney General in New Hampshire, and founding director of the NH Criminal Practice Clinic, a collaboration between the New Hampshire Public Defender's office and University of NH School of Law. She also served for ten years on the New Hampshire Adult Parole Board.

Other academic areas of expertise include Criminal and Juvenile Law.

Summary of Contents

Table of Contents

Acknowledgments

I am grateful to so many people who helped me. My research assistants, Lindsay Whitelaw and Greg Seidner, not only helped with many of the sections, they also "vetted" the book by providing the student's perspective that was vital to the book's mission. Many colleagues and friends read drafts, edited, supported, or encouraged the project. In particular, Professors Risa Evans, Jessica Durkis-Stokes, Kimberly Kirkland, Erin Corcoran, Sue Zago, Calvin Massey, Michael Vorenberg, Melissa Greipp, and Sam and Kate Alberts read drafts and provided invaluable feedback. My assistant, Deborah Paige, kept me from pulling my hair out on more than one occasion. I have been well supported by the University of New Hampshire School of Law's administration. Kate Spoto, a former colleague and current practitioner, read a draft and gave me critical advice from the lawyer's perspective.

The crew at Wolters Kluwer have been wonderful. My gratitude to Christine Hannan, Carol McGeehan, Dana Wilson, and Julie Nahil, copyeditor. To my family, Jill Alberts, Eliza Vorenberg, Roger Wellington, Nathan, Kathryn, and Gabriel Maggiotto, you have been patient, interested, and encouraging. And finally, to my fellow "writer" friends, Meg Cadoux Hirshberg and Lindley Shutz, if it were not for your initial push to put me onto this project, I would never have done it.

I would also like to acknowledge Thomson Reuters for granting permission to reprint materials:

Thomson Reuters, Westlaw headnotes to *Diaz v. Krob* (1994), *Rust v. Reyer* (1998), *Reickert v. Misciagna* (2002), and *Guercia v. Carter* (2000). Reprinted from Westlaw with permission of Thomson Reuters.

Thomson Reuters, McKinney's Consolidated Laws of New York Annotated, General Obligation Law, Chapter 24-A, §11-100. Reprinted from West Reporters with permission of Thomson Reuters.

PREPARING FOR PRACTICE

PART I

LEGAL WRITING
Learning a New Language

CHAPTER 1

Introduction

A. WE'RE NOT IN KANSAS ANYMORE

You have arrived at law school with solid writing ability. After all, you would not be here without them. Legal writing, however, requires some unique skills. In many ways, learning legal writing is more like acquiring a new language. It is important to remember this because there will be times when you will say to yourself: "I thought I was a good writer. Why is this so much harder than my undergraduate research papers?" When these moments hit, remind yourself that legal writing is a genre you are not yet accustomed to.

First, in legal writing, less is more. Good legal writing means getting to the point quickly. This usually means that you start with your conclusion, so your reader understands where he or she is headed, and that you use short sentences and manageable paragraphs so the reader moves easily through your writing. If you were a political science major, or a student of humanities, this style may seem backward to you. Legal writing is focused on the reader, whereas academic writing is a product that reflects self-discovery. In legal writing, you are always asked to put yourself in the place of the reader.

Second, in many law practices, time is money. Written communication must therefore be done in the most efficient manner possible. Whether you are writing to a client, a colleague in your office, or an opposing counsel, you will likely be mindful that the time you spend researching and writing will cost the client money. The challenge is to never sacrifice quality and accuracy for expediency.

Third, long gone are the days of "heretofore" and the "party-of-the-first-part." Effective legal writing uses plain English. Writing like a lawyer means using language and structure that a client can understand. Colleagues and judges may grasp the legal lingo better than clients, but they do not have the time or the patience to decipher complex words and dense paragraphs.

Finally, and perhaps most importantly, legal writing is a bit of a mischaracterization. You are actually learning how to analyze law and communicate about it effectively. That means that even before you learn how to write effectively, you must study and understand the law. Your legal writing class is about analyzing as much as it is about writing.

Consider yourself a student of a new language, a new way of communicating. Do not despair if your excellence in writing before law school does not seem to translate automatically into excellence in your first semester of law school. Be patient and you will soon see that, with guidance, the skills you have are indeed transferable to legal writing.

B. YOUR LEGAL WRITING CLASS

You will probably notice that your legal writing class doesn't look like your other first-year classes. Your legal writing class will be smaller. The book will be different, as it will likely be shorter and organized more like a reference book or textbook as opposed to a case book. The syllabus may look different. You will notice that you have more assignments due and that the course information for the class contains requisites for formatting, rubrics, or professionalism guidelines.

Remember, the first-year legal writing class is the first time you will get to act like a lawyer. In legal writing you learn law in the context of a hypothetical client's problem. You will communicate your analysis of the problem and your solution in written documents. If you were in medical school this class would be the first "clinical" course, where you learn the basics of assessing a patient by interviewing and examining a mock patient.

You will also receive a lot of feedback from your professor. Perhaps for the first time in your life, you will receive detailed input about analysis, organization, grammar, and style. At first, this may come as a bit of a shock, but this is where you learn to transfer those solid writing skills you brought to law school into masterful legal writing. You would not be human if you did not wince a little (or a lot) when you receive copious feedback. Keep in mind that the feedback is not personal; its only purpose is to help you become an effective lawyer. You and your professor share exactly the same goal—that you succeed as a legal writer.

You could be in a legal office as early as next summer. It is better to make mistakes now and work through them with your professor than to make them when you are in the "real" world. Being open to criticism and willing to work with your professor as a team will help you get the most out of your legal writing class.

C. CITATION? I HAVE TO LEARN THAT TOO?

You will notice that the cases you read for your other first-year classes rely on many kinds of authority, including other cases, statutes, and secondary sources, like the Restatement of Torts. Judges and lawyers use a uniform system of legal citation so that readers can easily find the authorities relied upon in documents. The citation system is governed by very particular rules. The *Bluebook* or the *ALWD Citation Manual* are the books you will use as references for citing accurately. You will likely use these books during and after law school, so hold on to them!

When you refer to cases, statutes, or other authorities in your legal writing, you will use the same type of uniform system and you will also have the *Bluebook* or the *ALWD Citation Manual* as your references. At first, the citation rules will seem mysterious and very persnickety. With practice, though, you will get used to the rules, become adept at learning how to cite, and the endeavor will become second nature to you. Again, be patient.

D. WHAT DO I NEED TO DO TO SUCCEED AT LEGAL WRITING?

The phrase legal writing professors hear over and over again during the first weeks of the semester is, "I can't believe how much time it takes to write a short memo!" Thus, the number one piece of advice is: Don't underestimate the time it takes to do the assignment. While waiting until the last minute may have worked when you were an undergraduate, it is unlikely to work in law school. Even a short, three-page assignment can take longer than you think it will.

The way to succeed in legal writing is as follows:

- Start early—plan ahead.
- Read the directions—know what is being asked.
- Meet with your professor and your teaching assistant.
- Learn to *study* (not just read) the law.
- Revise.
- Revise.
- Revise again.

Because learning about legal writing is like learning a new language, it will help if you are willing to make mistakes and learn from them. Becoming an effective legal analyst and writer is a **recursive** process. With each new assignment, you will have a chance to practice a skill you have already tried and learn new ones. Stay open to retrying, rethinking, and revising!

E. HOW THIS TEXTBOOK IS ORGANIZED

After this introduction and the first five chapters, this textbook has three case files. A case file contains the information you will need to solve the client's problem. The assigning memorandum and accompanying documents mirror the kind of information you are likely to be given in practice. With each case file, you will learn new skills and practice old ones. This book is set up to review acquired skills and introduce new ones as the book progresses into more complex legal problems.

The case files are meant to look like what you would work on in practice. They are also similar to the Multi-State Performance Test (MPT). The MPT is the bar exam testing format used by most states. A typical MPT includes a file and a library. The file consists of source documents containing all the facts of the case. The specific assignment is described in a memorandum from a supervising attorney. The file might also include transcripts of interviews, depositions, hearings or trials, pleadings, correspondence, client documents, contracts, newspaper articles, medical records, police reports, or lawyer's notes. The library includes the legal authorities, such as cases or statutes. The case files in this textbook look similar (though not identical) to the file and library contained in an MPT.

Throughout the book, you will see "On Your Own" exercises. Your professor may assign some or all of these and require you to prepare the answers. If not, I suggest you do the exercises. Each one is designed to test your understanding and give you an opportunity to practice the skills covered.

CHAPTER 2

How (and Why) Do Lawyers Communicate?

A. WRITING TO EXPLAIN: THE PREDICTIVE ANALYSIS

Imagine that you have completed your first year of law school. You have an internship or a paid job with a firm, a government agency, a nonprofit organization, or a corporation. One of your new colleagues, perhaps your supervisor, asks you to find out the answer to a legal question that pertains to a client's case. She asks you to draft "something" that sets out the law on the particular question and also how the law might affect the client's situation.

The reason she is asking you to draft this information is likely because she is either deciding whether to pursue the client's case on this issue, or she has decided to take the case but wants to know everything about the issue before she drafts the complaint or writes a brief. Your colleague wants to be educated about the issue, not persuaded to go one way or the other.

What do you do? First, you read the client's file (or whatever documents your colleague has given you), then you research the issue. Once you have a good idea of what the law is, you draft an outline and a legal memorandum. She may have asked you to e-mail her the results of your research.

Whether it is in an e-mail or a memorandum, the task is the same and the format is the same. You will begin with a statement of the issue followed by a brief answer (or summary) that addresses the particular issue. You may include a statement of the facts of the client's case, then you write the discussion. This is where you explain the law and then apply the law to the client's problem.

Here is an example of what might happen when you are asked to write a predictive legal analysis. Let's say you are working in a firm and your supervisor tells you that one of her clients, whom she represents primarily on business matters, has been accused of shoplifting. It turns out that the client has had similar trouble before. The lawyer is preparing to take the case to trial and wants to know if evidence of the client's prior misdeeds will be relevant (and thus potentially admissible) in the client's trial. She asks that you research and advise her on whether the evidence is legally relevant under state law.

What follows is an example of the predictive analysis you might return to her:

MEMORANDUM

To: Attorney Supervisor
From: Student Lawyer
Date: September 15, 20XX
Re: *State v. Albert*: Criminal Theft—Relevance of Albert's prior shoplifting, #CR23456

Issue

In Maureen Albert's trial for theft of a ham from a Hannaford Supermarket (*Hannaford*), is evidence of a prior incident relevant where in the prior case Albert removed a turkey from the same Hannaford without paying?

Brief Answer

Probably yes. Evidence of Albert's earlier shoplifting incident is probably relevant under New Hampshire Rule of Evidence 404(b). Admission of prior bad act evidence under Rule 404(b) requires that: (1) the evidence is relevant for a purpose other than showing the defendant's character, (2) there is clear proof that the defendant actually committed the prior act, and (3) the probative value of the evidence outweighs its prejudicial impact. As instructed, this memo addresses only the question of relevance. Albert has made her intent an issue by specifically claiming she removed the ham accidentally. The evidence of Albert's prior shoplifting is thus likely relevant to rebut her claim that she took the ham by accident.

Facts

In November 2011, three months before the current incident occurred, Maureen Albert left the Hannaford in Concord, New Hampshire without paying for a turkey that she had placed in the bottom of her cart. Albert returned the turkey, was warned about her behavior, and was not prosecuted.

In February 2012, Albert took a cart containing a spiral ham out of the same Hannaford without paying for it. When a Hannaford employee stopped her in the parking lot, Albert said that she left the store because she realized she had forgotten her wallet in her car. She stated that she did not intend to steal the ham and had removed it from the store accidentally.

The State has charged Albert with shoplifting for the second incident. In her trial, the State wants to introduce evidence of the turkey incident to prove that she intended to steal the ham.

Discussion

Albert's prior act involving the turkey is relevant for a purpose other than character because she raised the issue of intent, and the prior act is factually similar and close in time to the charged act. Evidence is relevant for a purpose other than character if it (1) has a direct bearing on an issue actually in dispute, and (2) a clear and logical connection exists between that act and the crime charged. *McGlew*, 658 A.2d at 1194. The trial court must make specific findings on each of these elements. *Id.*

1. Direct Bearing on Issue in Dispute

Evidence of a prior act is relevant to refute a defendant's claim that the crime was committed by accident. *Lesnick*, 677 A.2d at 690. For example, the court in Lesnick admitted evidence of defendant's prior bad act because it was relevant to show the absence of an accident. *Id.* Specifically, the defendant claimed she stabbed her husband in self defense, believing him to be an unknown intruder. *Id.* In contrast, where the defendant denied any involvement at all in the crime, the court excluded the evidence. *State v. Blackey*, 623 A.2d 1333, 1334 (N.H. 1993). It reasoned that the evidence was not relevant because, by denying the crime altogether, the defendant had not placed her intent or propensity at issue. Id. at 1334; *State v. Whittaker*, 642 A.2d 936, 938 (N.H. 1994).

Albert's prior act is likely relevant here because she claims she took the ham by accident. Like the defendant in *Lesnick*, who admitted the stabbing but claimed it was an accident, Albert made her intent an issue by claiming she took the ham unintentionally. Evidence of a prior similar act is relevant to disproving Albert's claim of accident. Because the evidence of the prior act is offered for a purpose other than Albert's character or propensity to steal meat, it is probably admissible.

2. Clear and Logical Connection

Next, the evidence probably meets the second prong of the relevancy analysis because a clear, logical connection exists between the charged act of stealing a ham and the prior act of taking a turkey. A clear, logical connection exists where the acts are factually similar, and the prior act is "not so remote in time as to eliminate the nexus" between the prior act and the crime charged. *McGlew*, 658 A.2d at 1194. The State must articulate a precise chain of reasoning between the prior act and the charged act without relying on inferences about the defendant's character, which are forbidden. *Id.* at 1195. For example, in *Lesnick*, a logical connection existed between the prior stabbing and the charged stabbing because the defendant committed each crime under similar emotional circumstances against the same victim using the same weapon. *Id.* The factual similarities between the two acts permitted the conclusion that the defendant intended the second act since two identical "accidents" within a few months were unlikely. *Id.*

Where two acts are significantly different, the court will not admit evidence of the first one to prove the defendant's intent in committing the second act. In *McGlew*, the State failed to establish a nexus between a prior accusation of sexual molestation and the charged act of sexual assault because the prior act, which occurred six years earlier, involved a victim of a different age and gender and a different sex act. 658 A.2d at 1194. The factual differences between the two acts suggested that the defendant might have had differing intent during each. *See id.* (noting that the prior act was not relevant, although intent was an element of the charge).

In Albert's case, the turkey and the ham were similar products removed from the same store, using the same method of removal—all facts that show that the second incident was not an accident. Like *Lesnick*, where the close factual similarity between the prior act and the charged act made the prior act relevant to the defendant's intent, here the virtually identical facts probably make Albert's prior act relevant to her subsequent taking of the turkey.

Moreover, the close time frame between Albert's two incidents further strengthens their connection. The closer the temporal proximity between two acts, the more likely a court is to find that the actor had the same intent at both times. *See Lesnick*, 677 A.2d at 690 (emphasizing the temporal proximity of the charged act and the prior act). In *Lesnick*, the prior act was relevant because it occurred only two months before the charged crime, whereas in *McGlew*, the prior crime was not admitted, in part, because it occurred six years earlier. 658 A.2d at 1194. Similar to *Lesnick*, who committed the two acts within two months, Albert committed the two acts within three months. Although a person may make one mistake, she is unlikely to make two identical mistakes within a few months. The short time between Albert's two acts supports their logical connection. Because the prior act demonstrates Albert's intent, the court probably will find that the evidence meets the relevancy requirement of the three-part test.

Albert's only argument in her favor likely relies on the underlying purpose of 404(b). She could argue that allowing the bad act evidence against her goes against the purpose behind 404(b) and its limitations. *Id.* at 1195 (holding purpose underlying Rule 404(b) is to ensure that a defendant is tried on the merits of the case and not on character). However, the concern that a defendant not be convicted on the basis of character is met where, as here, there is a sufficient, specific purpose for its admission. By claiming that she mistakenly took the turkey, Albert has placed her own intent to commit theft at issue. The prosecutor would probably be successful in arguing that the purpose of the evidence is to refute that claim and not to demonstrate her bad character.

Notice that the memorandum is an informative document that explains and applies the law and predicts that the prior evidence will come in as evidence in a trial against the client. The memorandum also includes a short counter-analysis at the end. This tells the reader that you have considered the opposing arguments and legal analysis. It also gives the reader a full picture of the legal issue. Remember that the memorandum is supposed to be a thorough and accurate analysis so that your supervisor can decide the best course of action; therefore, it is important that any weaknesses in the case be addressed. This information will be critical to your supervisor, who will use it to advise the client on whether to take a plea in the case or go to trial.

B. WRITING TO INTERPRET: WRITING ABOUT LAW (NOT RELATED TO A CLIENT'S FACTS)

Predictive legal writing can take other forms. For instance, you may be asked to interpret a statute or explain a new case that has just come down. A predictive memorandum could also be used to prepare for a settlement negotiation or a decision not to file a complaint. Or you may be asked to explain a statute or legal principle. For example, imagine that the firm or business where you are working has several clients who are landlords. A new version of a tenant eviction process has just been enacted. You have been asked to interpret the steps necessary to evict a tenant under the statute.

Here is an example of what your response would look like:

MEMORANDUM

To: Supervisor
From: Student Lawyer
Date: August 2, 20XX
Re: New Hampshire Eviction Process

Question:

    What steps are required to initiate and carry out eviction proceedings for a tenant who has not paid rent?

Summary of Relevant Law:

    The eviction process in NH is a multi-step process set out in N.H. Rev. Stat. Ann. §540 and District Court Rule 5. First, the landlord must make a demand for rent. If no rent is paid then the landlord can file a Notice to Quit. The tenant is entitled to a hearing to challenge the demand. At the hearing, if the landlord sustains a claim of unpaid rent, the judge can order the tenant to pay back rent and a writ of possession that authorizes a sheriff to remove the tenant from the premises.

Steps to Evict a Tenant:

    1. Demand for Rent

    First, the landlord must make a demand for rent from the tenant. N.H. Rev. Stat. Ann. §540:3-4. The demand must state the amount owed and it must be served on the tenant personally or left at the residence. Either way, the landlord must show proof of the service by an attested copy of the demand and an affidavit that sets out that service was made. N.H. Rev. Stat. Ann. §540:5. The district court clerk's office has the forms needed; however, the landlord is not required to use the forms. N.H. Rev. Stat. Ann. §540:5.

    2. Notice to Quit

    The landlord must also provide the tenant with a written Notice to Quit (also called an "eviction notice"). N.H. Rev. Stat. Ann. §540:2(I). This can be done at the same time as the demand for rent. The Notice must be in writing and must state the specific reason for the eviction. N.H. Rev. Stat. Ann. §540:3(I-III)). When the reason for termination of tenancy is nonpayment of rent, 30 days' notice of eviction is sufficient. N.H. Rev. Stat. Ann. §540:3(II). The Notice to Quit must also inform the tenant that the tenant can avoid eviction by paying the past rent plus $15 in liquidated damages. N.H. Rev. Stat. Ann. §540:3(II), (III); 540:9.

    3. Service of the Notice to Quit

    The landlord can either serve the Notice to Quit personally with the tenant, or leave it at the tenant's residence. NH. Rev. Stat. Ann. §540: 5. Like the rule for the demand for rent, the landlord must show proof of the service by an attested copy of the Notice and an affidavit that sets out that service was made. The district court clerk's office has the forms needed. The landlord is not required to use the forms so long as all the information is on the notice. N.H. Rev. Stat. Ann. §540:5.

4. Writ of Summons

If the tenant has not complied with the demand for rent or the Notice to Quit, the landlord can go to the district court clerk's office and ask that the court issue a Writ of Summons. N.H. Rev. Stat. Ann. §540:13. Once the Writ is issued, a sheriff will serve the Writ and the tenant will have seven days to either leave the premises or request a hearing by filing an appearance at the district court. N.H. Rev. Stat. Ann. §540:13(II)(d)(1).

5. The Court Hearing

If the tenant requests a hearing, the court will schedule one within ten days after the date of the tenant's appearance is filed. N.H. Rev. Stat. Ann. §540:13(V). Both the tenant and the landlord are entitled to discovery prior to the hearing pursuant to N.H. Dist. Ct. R. 5.6. N.H. Rev. Stat. Ann. §540:13 (IV). At the hearing, the landlord would present the case for the unpaid rent and show proof of the demand and Notice to Quit. The tenant is allowed to present evidence in defense. N.H. Rev. Stat. Ann. §540:13(III). The court will decide the matter and can award the landlord the unpaid rent up to $1,500.

If the tenant does not file an appearance, the court will send a notice of default to the tenant within three days of issuing a Writ of Possession. N.H. Rev. Stat. Ann. §540:14(I). Once the Writ of Possession is issued the sheriff is authorized to remove the tenant from the premises.

Notice that this memorandum is purely about the law. There is no application of the law to a client's problem.

Predictive writing is typically done "in house," meaning that it is done for internal use. In other words, it is done within a law office or by a clerk in a judge's chambers. Because this type of legal writing is done to inform and educate and not to persuade, there is little likelihood of writing an objective analysis in a brief for a court. That is where persuasive legal writing comes in.

C. WRITING TO PERSUADE: THE PERSUASIVE MEMORANDUM OR BRIEF

Now imagine that you have completed your first year of law school and you are working in a state prosecutor's office. You are asked to draft a persuasive motion *in limine* arguing that the prior evidence regarding Albert's removal of the turkey from the supermarket should be admissible in a trial against her for the theft of the ham.

The format and content of persuasive legal writing is similar to objective writing. However, instead of informing the reader, the task is to *convince* the reader that whatever position you want the court to take is supported and thus should prevail. The tone (language) used will be slightly different. Notice in the example below how similar the structure and content of the memorandum is to the predictive memorandum.

STATE OF NEW HAMPSHIRE

MERRIMACK, SS.   SEPTEMBER TERM 2013

SUPERIOR COURT

State of New Hampshire

v.

Maureen Albert

No. 000-2013-CV-0000

STATE'S MOTION *IN LIMINE* TO ADMIT EVIDENCE OF OTHER BAD ACTS

NOW COMES the State of New Hampshire, by and through its attorney, Leslie Witman of the Office of the State Prosecutor, and hereby seeks an order from this Court admitting evidence to trial regarding Defendant Maureen Albert's (hereinafter "Albert" or "Defendant") prior bad act of shoplifting a turkey from a Hannaford Supermarket.

INTRODUCTION

Defendant's prior bad act of shoplifting is admissible under New Hampshire Rule of Evidence 404(b) because it is relevant to show Defendant's intent, not mere character evidence; there is clear proof that the Defendant actually committed the act; and the probative value of the evidence outweighs any prejudicial impact on a jury. As previously stipulated, this motion addresses only the first question of relevance.

Defendant is currently charged with theft of a ham from a Hannaford Supermarket in Concord, New Hampshire in February 2012, just three months after a similar incident in which Defendant shoplifted a turkey from the same store. By claiming that she did not intend to steal the ham for which she is currently charged, Defendant put her own intent at issue. As such, Defendant's similar prior act is relevant to her state of mind at the time of the second shoplifting incident and ought to be admissible to rebut her claim that she stole the meat by mere accident.

In further support of its motion to admit this evidence at trial, the State says as follows:

BACKGROUND

Ms. Maureen Albert removed a turkey placed in the bottom of her shopping cart without paying from the Hannaford Supermarket in Concord, New Hampshire in November 2011. Albert returned the turkey after being confronted, was warned about her behavior, and was not prosecuted. Just three months later, in February 2012, Albert shoplifted a spiral ham using a shopping cart from the same store. When confronted by an employee in the parking lot, Albert stated that she left the store because she had forgotten her wallet in her car. She brought her state of mind into issue even further by also stating that she did not intend to steal the ham and had removed it from the store accidentally. The State has now charged Albert with shoplifting for the second offense.

ARGUMENT

Ms. Maureen Albert's prior act of taking a turkey from the Concord, New Hampshire Hannaford without paying is relevant to prove that she intended to shoplift the ham for which she is currently charged from the same store. When evidence has a direct bearing on an issue actually in dispute, and a clear and logical connection exists between that act and the crime charged, then the evidence is relevant for a purpose other than character. *McGlew*, 658 A.2d 1191, 1194. Albert's prior act is relevant to refute her claim that she took the ham accidentally. In addition, the prior act is factually similar and close in time because she removed meat without paying twice in three months from the same store.

1. Direct Bearing on Issue in Dispute

Albert's prior act of taking a turkey is relevant to refute her claim that shoplifting the ham was by accident. Generally, evidence of a prior act is relevant to refute a defendant's claim that the crime was committed by accident. *Lesnick*, 677 A.2d 686, 690 (N.H. 1996). For example, in *Lesnick*, where the defendant claimed she stabbed her husband in self-defense because she believed him to be an unknown intruder, the court admitted evidence of a prior act because it was relevant to show that absence of an accident. *Id.* In contrast, when a defendant denies any involvement in a crime, prior act evidence is excluded. *State v. Blackey*, 623 A.2d 1333, 1334 (N.H. 1993). By denying the crime altogether, the defendant in *Blackey* had not placed her intent or propensity at issue, so the prior act evidence was not relevant and the court excluded it. *Id.*

Albert's prior act is relevant because she claimed that she took the ham by accident. Similar to the defendant in *Lesnick*, who admitted to stabbing her husband but claimed it was by accident, Albert made her intent an issue by claiming she took the ham unintentionally when returning to her car. Evidence of her prior similar act is relevant to rebut Albert's claim of taking the ham by accident. Because the evidence of the prior removal of meat is not offered to show Albert's character or propensity, but rather to rebut her claim of mere mistake, it is admissible.

2. Clear and Logical Connection

Albert's prior act is also relevant because a clear, logical connection exists between the charged act of shoplifting a ham and the prior act of taking a turkey from the same store within three months of each other. Where the acts are factually similar, and the prior act is "not so remote in time as to eliminate the nexus" between the prior act and the crime charged, then a clear, logical connection exists. *McGlew*, 658 A.2d at 1194. Where a precise chain of reasoning between the prior act and the charged act exists, the prior evidence is admissible. *Id.* at 1195. In *Lesnick*, a logical connection existed between the prior stabbing and the charged stabbing because the defendant committed each crime under similar emotional circumstances against the same victim using the same weapon. *Id.* The factual similarities between the two acts concluded that the defendant intended the second act since two identical "accidents" within a few months of each other were unlikely. *Id.*

Albert's prior act and current charge are so significantly similar that a clear and logical nexus connects the two events. In *McGlew*, where a prior accusation of sexual molestation and the charged act of sexual assault, which occurred six years later, involved a different victim of different age and gender and a different sex act, the prior charge was inadmissible because there was not a sufficient nexus between the two acts. 658 A.2d at 1194. The factual differences could not permit the conclusion that the defendant had the same intent during each act and therefore the prior act was inadmissible. *Id.*

The virtually identical facts of Albert's two acts permit the conclusion that she intended the second act since two identical "accidents" within such a short time frame is unlikely. The turkey and ham were similar products removed from the same store, using the same method of removal—suggesting that the second shoplifting incident was intentional. Similar to the facts in *Lesnick*, where the close similarity of the two acts rendered the prior act relevant to the defendant's intent in stabbing her husband, here the virtually identical circumstances and facts permit the conclusion that Albert's prior act is also relevant to her intent to steal the ham.

In addition to the factual similarities of Albert's two acts, the time frame between the two shoplifting incidents further indicates that her intent was to steal the ham. When two acts are close in proximity, the more likely an actor had the same intent at both times. *See Lesnick*, 677 A.2d at 690 (emphasizing the temporal proximity of the charged act and the prior act). In *Lesnick*, the prior act was relevant because it occurred only two months before the charged crime, whereas in *McGlew*, the prior act committed six years earlier was not admitted. 677 A.2d at 690; 658 A.2d at 1194. Albert's prior removal of a ham and subsequent shoplifting of a turkey just three months later is similar to Lesnick, who committed the two acts within two months. Although a person may make one mistake, she is unlikely to make two nearly identical mistakes within such a short time. The close proximity in time between Albert's two acts further supports their logical connection and renders her prior act of shoplifting relevant. Because the prior act demonstrates Albert's intent, and is not mere character or propensity evidence, it is relevant to the current charge.

Albert's argument that allowing the bad act evidence against her goes against the purpose behind 404(b) and its limitations is without merit. The concern that a defendant not be convicted on the basis of character is met where, as here, there is a sufficient, specific purpose for its admission. By claiming that she mistakenly took the turkey, Albert has placed her own intent to commit theft at issue. Thus, the purpose of the evidence is to refute Albert's claim of accident, and not to demonstrate her bad character.

WHEREFORE the State of New Hampshire respectfully requests that this Honorable Court:

A. Find that evidence of Defendant's prior act of taking a turkey from the Concord, New Hampshire Hannaford in November 2011 is admissible at Albert's trial; and

B. Grant such other and further relief as this Court deems just and proper.

Respectfully submitted,
THE STATE OF NEW HAMPSHIRE
By its attorney,

Date: September 22, 2013 By: /s/ Leslie Witman
Leslie Witman
NH Bar # 000
Assistant County Attorney
County Prosecutors Bureau
3 Main Street
Concord, NH 03301

CERTIFICATE OF SERVICE

I hereby certify on this 22nd day of September 2013, copies of the foregoing Motion *In Limine* were sent by e-mail to Maureen Albert and her counsel.

/s/ Leslie Witman, Esq
Leslie Witman, Esq

D. WRITING TO A CLIENT: COMMUNICATING TO A LAYPERSON

Communicating with clients makes up a lot of what lawyers do. Typically, lawyers write to clients to keep them updated and to explain to them the legal, practical, and procedural ramifications of their cases. Client letters (which are often done in e-mails) can also memorialize decisions that clients have made, such as to settle a case or proceed to court. In addition, client letters may address whether a client wants to agree to a contract term.

While some clients will be lawyers, most legal correspondence is between a lawyer and a non-lawyer. This book, and most legal writing instruction, will demand that you always write in plain English. However, the need for clarity is especially critical when writing to a client.

Here is an example of a client letter that Albert's lawyer might send her regarding whether she should plead guilty to a reduced sentence and avoid a trial. Notice the absence of specific references to cases.

Maureen Albert
3 Pike Street
Concord, New Hampshire

Re: Shoplifting case

Dear Ms. Albert:

As requested, I am writing to give you my opinion on whether you should accept the prosecutor's offer of a misdemeanor plea and a probationary sentence. As you and I discussed, the key question is whether your prior incident at the same Hannaford will come into the trial as evidence. If the judge allows the evidence, the likelihood of a not guilty verdict diminishes. This letter will address why the prior incident will likely be allowed into evidence.

Explanation of Relevant Law

As I explained to you at our meeting, evidence of prior similar activity is allowed to come into a trial under certain limited circumstances. The prior incident must be relevant for a purpose other than just to show character. In other words, the prior incident must have a direct bearing on the current case and there must be a clear, logical connection between the prior incident and the current case. Thus, the judge can allow prior evidence of similar conduct if the prosecutor can prove that the evidence is relevant and that there is a logical reason to do so.

Your Case

The prosecutor will argue that the incident involving the ham should be allowed at your trial because it involves very similar conduct and it shows that you didn't take the turkey by accident. In your trial, the prosecutor will have to prove that you had an intent to steal the turkey. She will argue that, by claiming that the turkey removal was an accident, you have put your intent at issue, which, she will say, opens the door for her to put in evidence of the ham incident. She will argue that your claim of accident can be refuted because you did a similar act recently. In addition, she will argue that the two scenarios are so similar and close in time that you could not have removed the turkey by accident.

I think that there is a good chance that the judge will allow evidence of your prior incident to come into the trial. Because the acts are so similar and close in time, the judge will probably find that the jury can use the evidence as proof that you did not take the turkey by accident. We will argue that this evidence would unfairly prejudice the jury against you and there is law we can use to support this argument. However, my belief is that the judge will not rule in our favor.

Conclusion and Next Steps

The prosecutor has offered one year of probation in exchange for your guilty plea to the theft. Whether to accept this offer is entirely up to you. If you decide to reject the offer, I will do my best to represent you at trial. It can be hard to predict what a jury will do. However, given the likelihood that the judge will allow the prior incident to come into evidence, I think it will be difficult, though not impossible, to get a not guilty verdict. If you were to go to trial, the judge could give you a longer probationary sentence, deferred jail time, or actual jail time (though I think this is unlikely). Given what you have told me about your need to care for your family and your desire to put this incident behind you, I would advise that you accept the prosecutor's offer. I am happy to discuss this further. I know it is a big decision and you want to feel as though you are making the right choice.

Please call my office and set up a time to go over this information and any questions you have.

Sincerely,

Lawyer

There are, of course, many other kinds of writing that you will do: drafting legislation, making notes to a file, writing judicial opinions (if you are a judicial law clerk or become a judge), writing contracts and legal documents, and perhaps writing scholarly pieces. And in law school (and on the bar exam), you will be writing exam answers. The skills you learn in your legal writing class will help you be an effective writer in all of these situations.

CHAPTER 3

Where Does the Law We Use Come From?

Learning to write effectively as a lawyer means you will need to be a good and careful analyzer of the law. In the United States, law comes from many sources, and in this chapter we review those sources.

You will notice that in your other courses, like Torts and Civil Procedure, many of the cases you read are appellate opinions. Appellate opinions come from courts that review the decisions of lower courts and administrative bodies. Appellate opinions make good vehicles for learning law because they often summarize and apply important legal concepts. You will also read cases from trial level courts. Typically, these cases address pretrial issues, such as decisions on motions on evidentiary issues and motions to dismiss. Often a case will settle after a court has ruled on a pretrial motion.

Keep in mind that the opinions you read are often the last chapter of a legal issue that began with a client's problem. The case probably started where most cases start: when a client goes to see a lawyer for help. Clients come in all shapes and sizes, including individuals, corporations, state agencies, or nonprofit organizations. When a client comes to a lawyer, it is typically to solve a problem or answer a question. The first step for the lawyer is to figure out what laws will determine the solutions or answers.

Let's say that a 60-year-old woman comes to a lawyer because she has been fired and she thinks her employer was wrong. She suspects she is being discriminated against on the basis of her age and has evidence to support her suspicion. How do you figure out whether it was legally wrong? You will have to learn if there are state or federal statutes or regulations that govern employment matters. Perhaps there are court opinions from the state or federal courts. There may be regulations promulgated by state or federal agencies that prohibit termination on the basis of age. In other words, understanding what makes up our system of rules and laws is critical to being a lawyer.

Most lawyers end up specializing in one area of law. With experience, the statutes, cases, regulations, and practices in the area in which you specialize will become familiar to you. As a newcomer to the field, it will help you, no matter which area of practice you eventually choose, to understand the overall framework of our system of laws.

The U.S. Constitution is the highest law of the land. The Constitution establishes a power-sharing form of government between the national (federal) government and state governments, known as federalism. This is different from a centralized system of power, such as that practiced in France or the United Kingdom.

The Constitution enumerates the powers of the federal government and reserves the non-enumerated powers to the state governments. The states are supreme in matters reserved to them, although there is very little that is expressly reserved to states because their power begins only where valid federal authority ends. For those matters that are reserved to the states, such as establishing local governments or regulating intra-state commerce, each state is sovereign and eligible to make and interpret its own laws without any interference from other states and the federal government. As a result, each of the 50 states has its own constitution, statutes, and other forms of law.

Keep in mind that all provisions of the state constitution must comply with the U.S. Constitution and federal statutory law. For instance, a state constitution cannot deny an accused criminal the right to a jury trial because the U.S. Constitution would prohibit such a law. The Supremacy Clause of the U.S. Constitution provides that federal law is superior to state law.

What follows is a brief civics review (for purposes of background and foundation) and a general summary of how the law is structured in the United States.

There are three branches of government in the United States: the legislative, the judiciary, and the executive. All three branches make law. Every state has the same structure with three branches that also make law.

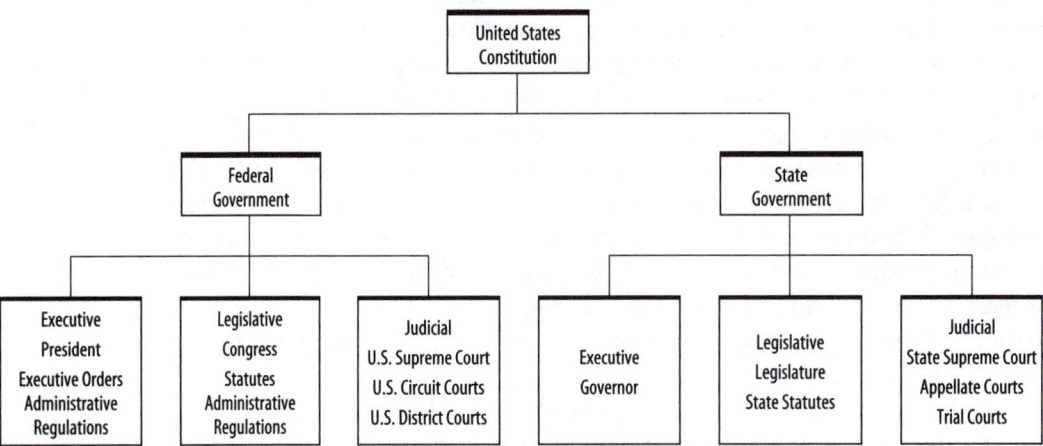

A. THE EXECUTIVE BRANCH

1. The Federal Executive

a. Federal Regulations

Because Congress cannot legislate with the detail necessary to implement all its laws, the executive branch creates administrative agencies that implement federal law (such as the U.S. Department of Agriculture). Congress often provides agencies the authority to promulgate rules and regulations that execute the federal law. These regulations, as well as proposed regulations, are recorded in the *Federal Register*, a daily publication that reports the daily activities of the executive branch. When these regulations are made final, they are codified in the *Code of Federal Regulations (CFR)*, a collection of all the regulations currently in force put in order of subject.

For example, in 1946 Congress passed the National School Lunch Program (NSLP), which reimburses schools for the cost of providing free and reduced lunch to its income-eligible students. In order to inform schools and the public about how the NSLP works, the U.S. Department of Agriculture (the agency created by the executive branch to make policy on farming, agriculture, and food), promulgated regulations that specified the program details. Here is an excerpt from a regulation:

> (i) *Requirements for lunch.* School lunches offered to children age 5 or older must meet, at a minimum, the meal requirements in paragraph (b) of this section. Schools must follow a food-based menu planning approach and produce enough food to offer each child the quantities specified in the meal pattern established in paragraph (c) of this section for each age/grade group served in the school. In addition, school lunches must meet the dietary specifications in paragraph (f) of this section. Schools offering lunches to children ages 1 to 4 and infants must meet the meal pattern requirements in paragraph (p) of this section. 7 CFR 210.10

b. Legislation Proposals

The executive branch proposes many of the bills that are considered by Congress. Similarly, a state's executive branch proposes bills that are considered by state legislators.

c. Executive Orders

Article II of the U.S. Constitution grants to the president certain broad powers, including the power to issue executive orders. These orders, also called presidential directives, are effectively laws, but they do not need to be approved by Congress. Executive orders can be challenged in court, and legal scholars argue about the extent of presidential power to issue orders. The orders are numbered and recorded in the *Federal Register* and the *CFR.*

2. The State Executive

a. Legislation Proposals

A state's executive branch can draft proposals for consideration by the state's legislature.

b. State Regulations

Similar to the federal regulatory process, a state's executive branch creates administrative agencies pursuant to statutory authority (i.e., from the legislative branch). These agencies issue administrative regulations.

c. Executive Orders

State governors have the power to make executive orders. These orders are not laws and do not require legislative approval, but they are binding.

B. THE LEGISLATIVE BRANCH

1. Federal Laws

The U.S. Constitution gives Congress (made up of the House and the Senate) enumerated powers to make laws. Article I of the Constitution specifies the matters on which Congress is allowed to legislate. Congress is not allowed to make laws relating to matters not listed in Article I. Current federal laws are organized by subject and put into the federal code (United States Code Annotated, abbreviated "U.S.C.A.").

2. State Laws

State constitutions give state legislatures the power to enact laws. If a state enacts a law relating to a matter reserved to the U.S. Congress by the Constitution and Congress passes a conflicting law, the state law will be preempted. Each state publishes its current laws in a code.

C. THE JUDICIAL BRANCH

1. Overview

The federal judicial branch includes the U.S. Supreme Court and lower federal courts. Every state has its own judicial branch that includes a state supreme court and inferior courts. Each system is responsible for deciding cases within its jurisdiction; the federal judiciary decides cases within the federal system and each state system decides cases within its state. The state and federal court systems operate parallel to one another, although the two systems can interact with one another; thus, the two systems are not completely independent.

Courts make law. They do this by upholding, interpreting, or striking down statutes that have been challenged, or by upholding or amending previous court decisions. Remember that a case usually begins in the lowest court (the trial court) and typically goes no further because it is either resolved or settled early. Generally, the decisions made by state trial court judges (called orders) are not published. They are written down and become a part of the court's case file. Some trial court order are published by online research services. Federal trial court opinions (which are longer than orders) are published.

Some cases are appealed to higher courts and it is in these decisions, which are recorded and published, that the courts make law. The appellate cases you read for your other courses all started with a client who had a problem. This case law makes up a large portion of the law that lawyers must use to help solve their clients' problems. Statutes make up the other portion of the law.

Legal cases fall into two main categories: civil and criminal. Civil cases are lawsuits to recover damages or to stop others from doing something. These are normally disputes among private individuals and businesses, though government institutions can also be party to civil actions. Conversely, criminal cases are lawsuits that seek punishment in the form of imprisonment or fine. In criminal cases, the government brings a lawsuit on behalf of the public against an individual who has violated a criminal law. In a civil suit, the party bringing the lawsuit is the plaintiff and the party defending the lawsuit is the defendant. In a criminal suit, the accused is called the defendant and the party bringing the case is called the state, the government, or the commonwealth.

2. The Federal Court System

The federal courts are only permitted to hear certain types of cases. The Constitution specifies the types of cases the U.S. Supreme Court can hear. When Congress created the federal trial courts and intermediate courts, it passed laws defining what types of cases the lower federal courts could hear.

Generally, the federal courts hear cases that involve questions of federal law, including the U.S. Constitution, federal statutes, cases in which the United States is a party, and cases involving U.S. citizens and citizens of other countries. They also hear state law cases between citizens of different states; however, they must apply state law. Cases at federal courts begin at the trial court level, which is called the U.S. District Court. Unsatisfied parties can appeal the decision to an appellate court, known as circuit court, and finally to the court of last resort, the U.S. Supreme Court. Congress has also established other inferior courts in the federal court system, such as bankruptcy and tax courts.

a. U.S. District Courts

The U.S. District Court is the lowest level of federal courts. This is where a litigant's case will usually enter the court system. The issue may involve a prior decision of an agency (e.g., the IRS). This is the only level in the lawsuit where parties have the chance to present evidence to support their claims. Judges determine issues of law and the jury examines the evidence of the parties (facts) and how those facts apply to the law. Ninety-four U.S. district courts exist in the United States, and every state has at least one.

The kinds of cases heard in a U.S. District Court include criminal cases involving violation of federal laws (e.g., kidnapping, bank robbery, or drug trafficking), civil cases involving claims that a federal law has been violated (e.g., the Constitution or U.S. treaties), civil cases between parties of different states alleging violation of state law for amounts in excess of $75,000 (these are cases brought under "diversity jurisdiction"), and civil actions brought by or against the United States. The U.S. District Court also hears appeals of certain federal agency decisions, such as Social Security Appeals Council decisions.

b. U.S. Circuit Courts of Appeals

The United States has 13 circuit courts. The federal circuit courts are appellate courts. The nation is divided geographically into 12 circuit boundaries, each with a circuit court. There is a thirteenth circuit that sits in Washington, D.C. A party dissatisfied with a district court ruling can appeal to the circuit court within his or her jurisdiction, except in criminal cases where the court finds the accused not guilty. There is no appeal of a not guilty verdict, and the case ends with the verdict. Generally, circuit courts do not review the facts of the cases that have come before them. They accept the facts that have been found by either a jury or a judge. Circuit courts examine whether mistakes exist in the lower court's decision about what the law is and how it applies to the facts of a given case. Hence, no additional evidence is taken at this stage. Occasionally, a circuit court will review facts, but only if there has been a clearly erroneous decision with regard to the facts. The court normally sits in panels of three judges.

c. U.S. Supreme Court

The U.S. Supreme Court is the highest court of the land and is located in Washington, D.C. The Supreme Court is also an appellate court. Parties unsatisfied with a circuit court decision or a state supreme court decision (if it involves federal law—more on that later) can petition the U.S. Supreme Court through a "petition for a writ of certiorari" to hear their case. Not all cases get to the Supreme Court. The Court decides to hear a case when four justices agree to hear it. The Court is made up of nine justices and, typically, all of the justices sit in all cases before the Court.

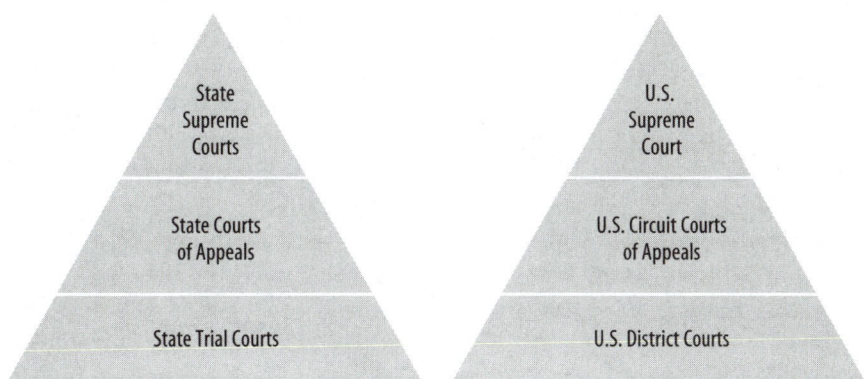

3. The State Court System

Like the federal system, most state courts have three levels of courts: a trial court where most lawsuits begin, an intermediate court, and the highest court. However, some states—including New Hampshire, Nevada, Montana, and Vermont, among others—have only two levels: a trial court and a supreme court.

a. Trial Courts

Almost all state courts have two kinds of trial courts: a court of limited jurisdiction that hears special cases (probate, family, juvenile, municipal, traffic matters, etc.) and a court that hears criminal and civil matters.

b. Intermediate Courts

Many, but not all, states have appellate courts between their trial courts and their highest court. Intermediate courts are normally based on districts or counties. Dissatisfied parties to a lawsuit in a trial court may appeal to an appropriate intermediate court. The intermediate courts of appeal generally deal with mistakes in the law and procedural errors made in the trial court. Occasionally, intermediate courts will review a lower court's findings of fact, but typically this occurs only when there is a clear error.

c. Highest State Court

Not all states call their highest courts "supreme courts." For instance, the highest courts in Maryland and New York are the court of appeals. Confusingly, New York calls its trial courts supreme courts. The highest courts of states without intermediate courts directly hear appeals from their trial courts. The highest state courts may have original jurisdiction in certain controversies. All cases in states end at this level, except in matters involving federal law where the U.S. Supreme Court has the final word. Most cases are never heard by the U.S. Supreme Court. Approximately 10,000 cases are submitted to the Court annually and only about 75 to 80 are accepted.

CHAPTER 4

How We Use the Law: Hierarchy of Law

Lawyers look for legal solutions to their clients' problems. The law or rules they look for depend on the facts of each client's case. Once a lawyer has identified the legal issue or issues that the client's problem fits into (e.g., age discrimination in employment; admission of a prior bad act in a criminal trial), the next step is to look for the law that will answer the problem. The law may come from constitutions, statutes, cases, regulations, or local ordinances, as discussed in Chapter 3.

There is a hierarchy of law: primary authority and secondary authority. Primary authority (the actual rules of law) carries more weight in resolving a legal issue than secondary authority (information about the law, such as law reviews or legal encyclopedias). The law you rely on to answer your client's problem will depend on several factors, such as what state you are in and whether the legal issue is addressed by federal or state law.

Primary authority can be either mandatory or persuasive. For example, if you are arguing a case in Nebraska, but one of the cases you are relying on is from Indiana, the Indiana case will be considered by the Nebraska court as primary authority (it contains actual rules), but it is not mandatory that the Nebraska court follow the case. This means that it will be persuasive, but not mandatory. In other words, some authority is decisive—you will have to follow it, and some is guiding—you can use it to shore up your position, but it isn't binding on the body deciding the legal question.

What follows is a summary of the precedential value that the different sources of law have. Keep in mind that your understanding of the sources and weight of law will become clearer when you are in the process of solving a client problem and have a context for what you are researching.

A. PRIMARY SOURCES OF LAW

Primary sources of law represent actual rules of law and are promulgated by entities that are empowered to create law, such as courts and legislatures. Constitutions, statutes, regulations, and cases are primary authority. Other sources may include court rules, municipal charters, and ordinances. Primary authority may be mandatory or persuasive. Mandatory authority is binding within a jurisdiction and, hence, courts must follow it. Conversely, persuasive authority does not bind courts in a jurisdiction but can influence a court's decision.

1. Constitutions

Constitutions are the highest laws of a land and therefore the most fundamental, authoritative sources of law. Typically, a state publishes its constitution in the beginning or the end of its statutory compilations. The U.S. Constitution is published in the United States Code (U.S.C.).

2. Statutes

State legislatures make statutes. Before laws become statutes, the legislature first enacts and publishes them as slip laws. Several slip laws are then compiled into session laws, which are later incorporated into statutory codes. The federal government has its own statutes. Federal statutes compilations include the United States Code (U.S.C.), United States Code Annotated (U.S.C.A.), and United States Code Service (U.S.C.S.).

3. Regulations

Regulations are agency-generated rules that have the force of law. Both federal and state agencies promulgate rules to implement and interpret certain statutory provisions. For example, the Family Educational Rights and Privacy Act of 1974 (FERPA) is a federal law designed to give parents or eligible students certain rights related to educational records. The U.S. Department of Education administers the laws and promulgates regulations to implement and enforce the law.

4. Judicial Opinions

Judicial opinions interpret statutes and regulations as well as prior cases. Thus, cases are next in the hierarchy authority after statutes and regulations. Because cases can be either mandatory or persuasive authority, prioritizing them in your citations is important. The general rule is that a state's supreme court cases within a jurisdiction are binding on all lower courts within that jurisdiction. For instance, all federal circuit courts and federal district courts must follow a decision (precedent) set by the U.S. Supreme Court. State courts must follow the ruling of the highest court of their state. However, a decision by the highest court of a state is only persuasive authority in courts of other states.

5. Mandatory Versus Persuasive Authority

Mandatory law *must* be followed by a court. Persuasive law *may* be followed by a court. In a state with an intermediate (appeals) court, a decision by the appellate court is binding on lower (trial) courts, but can only be persuasive in a litigant's case before the state's supreme court. An intermediate appeals court opinion provides persuasive authority to other intermediate appeals courts if a state has multiple mid-level appeals courts (e.g., in New York, there are four Appellate Division Courts). Such intermediate courts' opinions can also be persuasive in other states as well. In the federal system, a decision by a circuit court is only binding on lower courts within that circuit. For example, a decision by the First Circuit Court of Appeals is only binding in the U.S. District Courts of Maine, New Hampshire, Massachusetts, Puerto Rico, and Rhode Island. The opinions of one circuit court are persuasive authority to another circuit court and U.S. District Courts under other circuits.

Decisions by state trial courts and U.S. District Courts carry the least weight. A decision by a particular trial court or U.S. District Court in a jurisdiction is not binding on other trial courts in that jurisdiction. However, lower court opinions can be persuasive to other lower courts or even higher courts within its jurisdiction. This is especially true when a trial court has written an opinion that is exactly on point with an issue before another court. It is important to cite the authorities within a given jurisdiction based on the level of the court in that jurisdiction.

Judicial decisions are collected in reporters. Each state publishes its decisions in the reporters. Some of the reporters include the *North Eastern Reporter* and the *North Western Reporter,* among others.

Quite often, lawyers and judges turn to another state's law—especially case law—if their own state has not addressed a particular legal issue that the other state has. Sometimes lawyers or judges who have a case in federal court will look to state case law if there is no relevant federal case law on point. These situations all involve using persuasive authority rather than mandatory authority. The law used for support may be primary but is not binding and may be very helpful in deciding the issue because another court or legal body has already addressed it.

For example, recall the case about the 60-year-old woman who comes to you because she believes she was fired because of her age, not because she is incompetent. Let's say that your state has a state statute that prohibits discrimination based on age. That statute is primary authority that is also mandatory. Now imagine that you are gathering research and you find cases from your state's highest court that interpret the language of the statute. Those cases are also mandatory authority. In addition, you realize that *another* state has a very similar antidiscrimination statute as well as some cases that interpret that state's statute. Because the cases are interpreting a statute that is very similar to your state's statute, the cases have persuasive value. In other words, you can use the cases to shore up and support your position, but these cases have persuasive weight, not mandatory, binding weight.

The case that follows (*Diaz v. Krob*) is also an example where the parties and the court used other states' law to help decide an issue that had not yet been addressed in their own state. In the case, a woman was crossing a street when she stopped at the center median because the "Don't Walk" warning activated. A school bus driver stopped and motioned her to cross in front of the bus and, when she did so, the woman was struck and injured by a car. One issue in the case was whether the school bus driver had a duty to the woman whom he signaled (you will recognize the concept of "duty" from your Torts class). Notice in the paragraph beginning with a "6" where the court says, "The parties assert that the issue of whether a duty exists under the circumstances of this case is one of first impression in Illinois. The parties cite various out-of-state rulings in support of their respective positions." Because there are no similar cases in Illinois, the parties are using other states' case law (Michigan and New York) to persuade the court in Illinois to adopt their position. This is an example of primary authority (Michigan and New York case law) that is persuasive.

264 Ill.App.3d 97
Appellate Court of Illinois,
Third District.

Janet L. DIAZ and Jaime Diaz, wife and husband, Plaintiffs-Appellants,
v.
Grace KROB and Joliet Township High School District #204, Defendants-Appellees.
No. 3-93-0852. | June 30, 1994.

Pedestrian whom automobile struck after school bus driver motioned for pedestrian to cross street sued school district for negligence. The Circuit Court, 12th Judicial Circuit, Will County, Herman S. Haase, J., dismissed complaint. Pedestrian appealed. The Appellate Court, Breslin, J., held that defendants did not owe pedestrian duty.

Affirmed.

West Headnotes [Omitted....]

Opinion

Justice BRESLIN delivered the opinion of the court:

The plaintiffs, Janet L. Diaz and Jaime Diaz, filed this lawsuit against the defendants, Grace Krob (school bus driver) and Joliet Township High School District #204, for damages and loss of consortium from injuries Janet allegedly sustained when she was struck by an automobile after the school bus driver motioned for her to cross a street. The trial court dismissed the complaint finding that the defendants did not owe the plaintiffs a duty as a matter of law. We affirm.

The accident happened when Janet attempted to cross Collins Street, in Joliet, Illinois. The complaint alleged that as she proceeded west within the cross-walk, the "Don't Walk" warning sign activated. Thus, she stopped at the median dividing traffic on the street. At that point, the school bus driver, who was stopped immediately to the north of the crosswalk at the red light, motioned or waved to the plaintiff to continue walking across the street in front of the bus.

The complaint further alleged that the bus driver knew or should have known that the bus prevented the plaintiff from seeing traffic proceeding south on Collins Street in the lane nearest the curb. The complaint also alleged that as a proximate result of the bus driver's negligence in gesturing to the plaintiff to continue walking across the street the plaintiff suffered an injury when she was struck by a vehicle.

In response to these allegations, the defendants filed a motion to dismiss pursuant to section 2-615 of the Civil Practice Law (735 ILCS 5/2-615 (West 1992)) alleging that the plaintiffs failed to allege sufficient facts to give rise to a duty. The trial court agreed with the defendants and dismissed the complaint.

*99 [1] [2] A motion to dismiss under section 2-615 admits all well-pleaded facts in the complaint for purposes of the motion. (*Sisk v. Williamson County* (1994), 261 Ill.App.3d 49, 198 Ill.Dec. 342, 632 N.E.2d 672.) A cause of action will not be dismissed on the pleadings unless it clearly appears that no set of facts can be proved which will entitle **1233 ***801 the plaintiff to recover. (*Charles Hester Enterprises, Inc. v. Illinois Founders Insurance Co.* (1986), 114 Ill.2d 278, 102 Ill. Dec. 306, 499 N.E.2d 1319.)

[3] [4] [5] One of the necessary elements of a negligence cause of action is the existence of a duty which requires a person to conform to a certain standard of conduct for the purpose of protecting the plaintiff from an unreasonable risk of harm. (*Swett v. Village of Algonquin* (1988), 169 Ill. App. 3d 78, 119 Ill.Dec. 838, 523 N.E.2d 594; *Mitchell v. City of Chicago* (1991), 221 Ill. App.3d 1017, 164 Ill. Dec. 506, 583 N.E.2d 60.) It is not sufficient that the plaintiff's complaint merely alleges that a duty exists; the plaintiff must state facts from which the law will raise a duty. (*Swett,* 169 Ill.App.3d 78, 119 Ill.Dec. 838, 523 N.E.2d 594.) Factors relevant in determining whether a duty exists include: the foreseeability of injury, the likelihood of injury, the magnitude of the burden of guarding against the injury, the consequence of placing that burden on the defendant, and the possible seriousness of the injury. (*Deibert v. Bauer Brothers Construction Co.* (1990), 141 Ill.2d 430, 152 Ill.Dec. 552, 566 N.E.2d 239.) Whether a duty exists is a question of law to be determined by the court. *Mitchell,* 221 Ill. App.3d 1017, 164 Ill.Dec. 506, 583 N.E.2d 60.

[6] The parties assert that the issue of whether a duty exists under the circumstances of this case is one of first impression in Illinois. The parties cite various out-of-state rulings in support of their respective positions. (See *Sweet v. Ringwelski* (1961), 362 Mich. 138, 106 N.W.2d 742; *Peka v.*

Boose (1988), 172 Mich.App. 139, 431 N.W.2d 399; *Valdez v. Bernard* (1986), 123 A.D.2d 351, 506 N.Y.S. 2d 363.)

In *Sweet,* the Michigan Supreme Court held that the trial court should not have granted a directed verdict in favor of the defendant truck driver on the ground of no showing of negligence. The defendant truck driver had stopped his truck and waved for the ten-year-old plaintiff pedestrian to cross the street on the crosswalk in front of him. The plaintiff continued crossing the street into the lane next to the truck and was struck by a car. The court's decision was based on the fact that the plaintiff was only ten years old, that her vision may have been obscured by the defendant's truck, and that she relied on what she considered to be directions from an adult.

In *Peka,* the defendant motioned for a southbound motorist to make a left turn. The southbound motorist followed the defendant's signal and struck the plaintiff's vehicle. The Michigan Appellate Court found that the signaling motorist owed no duty to the plaintiff. *100 The court found that *Sweet* was easily distinguishable on the basis that it involved a ten-year-old child who relied on the directions of an adult. The court found that the *Sweet* case should be limited to its facts.

In *Valdez,* the plaintiff was injured when she crossed a street after a bus driver had motioned for her to do so. The New York court noted that under certain circumstances, a driver of a motor vehicle may be liable to a pedestrian where that driver undertakes to direct a pedestrian safely across the road in front of his vehicle and negligently carries out that duty. The court found, however, that the bus driver was not the proximate cause of the plaintiff's injury where the plaintiff interpreted the bus driver's wave to mean only that he would not move the bus while the plaintiff passed in front of it.

Applying the above-mentioned principles and case law, we hold that the trial court correctly found as a matter of law that the defendants did not owe the plaintiffs a duty under the facts of this case. Unlike the cases cited by the parties, the crosswalk at the intersection in question was controlled by a "Don't Walk" signal. Nonetheless, the instant plaintiff chose to ignore it and proceed across the remainder of the intersection. Unlike *Sweet,* the plaintiff was not a youngster who relied on the directions of an adult. While we agree that *Sweet* is good law, we do not go as far as *Valdez* where it is implied that a duty would exist if the plaintiff interpreted the bus driver's gesture as something more than an indication that the driver would not move the bus until the plaintiff passed.

We agree that an injury is foreseeable here. But whether a legal duty exists involves **1234 ***802 more than just foreseeability of possible harm; it also involves legal and social policies. (*Swett,* 169 Ill.App.3d 78, 119 Ill.Dec. 838, 523 N.E.2d 594.) Here, the magnitude of guarding against the injury and the consequence of placing that burden on the defendant weigh heavily in favor of finding no duty. An adult pedestrian with no obvious impairments should be held responsible for deciding whether gestures and directions given by a motorist can be safely followed. We simply do not believe that the instant bus driver's act of common courtesy should be transformed into a tort thereby giving the plaintiff license to proceed across an intersection against a warning light and without taking any precautions of her own.

For the forgoing reasons, the judgment of the circuit court of Will County is affirmed.

Affirmed.

B. SECONDARY SOURCES OF LAW

Secondary sources are scholarly works or compilations of sources that help explain the law; they are not laws in themselves. Such authorities may include encyclopedias, annotations, treatises, restatements of the law, and American Law Reports (A.L.R.), among others.

C. INTERNATIONAL LAW

Many of today's lawyers will end up practicing law on a global level. The international system of law is too large a topic to cover here and you will probably not have occasion to apply international law in your first year of law school. However, it is worth remembering that the U.S. legal system is one of many. Should your career in law involve practicing internationally, you may become familiar with sources of law like those that come from treaties that govern legal relationships between countries, the United Nations Charter, or the International Court of Justice. While the legal systems of most American states are based on common law, many countries, including France and Spain, follow a civil law system where the central source of law comes from codes and statutes. Religious law is another kind of legal system that is followed in countries such as Saudi Arabia and Iran. Many legal systems have a hybrid or combination of common and civil law or civil and religious law.

PART II

CASE FILE 1
Blake v. Weston

CHAPTER 5

Introduction to Case File 1

This textbook uses three different case files to teach you legal analysis and writing. Each case file will ask you to learn and practice skills that you will need as a lawyer. The case files become increasingly complex as you progress through the textbook. The learning is recursive. That is, each case uses and builds on the skills developed in earlier cases.

Case file 1 involves clients, a husband and wife, whose neighbors have threatened to sue them for damage to property caused by intoxicated teenagers attending the clients' teenage daughter's party. The party was at the clients' home and was hosted by the clients' daughter. The party occurred while the clients were away. For case file 1, will only be drafting the issue and discussion of an objective office memorandum, not the entire memorandum. Case files 2 and 3 will require that you write entire objective office memoranda. In the process of writing the issue and discussion for case file 1, you will learn the following skills:

- Reading and understanding a statute
- Close case reading
- Briefing a case
- Deconstructing and synthesizing case law to form a rule
- Identifying key client facts
- Structuring an office memorandum: parts of a memorandum
- Formulating and writing an issue
- Writing an outline of the discussion section
- Organizing an analysis, including explaining the rule and applying the rule
- Writing the legal discussion of an objective interoffice memorandum

MEMORANDUM

To: Student
From: Supervising Attorney
Date: August 23, 20XX
Re: **_Walter and Sarah Weston's Potential Social Host Liability_**

Our clients, Walter and Sarah Weston, whom we represent on several matters related to their business, have asked us to look into an unrelated legal issue. Their neighbors, the Blakes, have threatened to sue them for damage to a tree on their property. The damage was caused by several guests attending an underage drinking party at the Weston's home hosted by the Weston's 16-year-old daughter. The Westons haveasked us to look into their liability (and not whether their daughter, Alice, would be liable).

New York has a "Dram Shop" statute that imposes liability for injuries (including property damage) caused by intoxicated minors. Liability under this statute is imposed when alcohol is "furnished" by the defendant or when the defendant assisted in procuring alcoholic beverages for someone known or reasonably thought to be a minor. The Westons want to know if they can be held liable for damage caused by the intoxicated teenagers. Specifically, they want to know if the facts establish that they "furnished" alcohol even though they were not in attendance at the party. The pertinent facts follow.

On a Saturday night, the Weston's daughter, Alice, had a party at their house in Amherst, New York. During the party, several of the underage guests, who became intoxicated while at the party, took a saw from the Weston's house and went next door where they cut down a small pine tree in the front yard of the neighbors' house. It turned out that the tree was marking the grave of the neighbor's beloved show dog, "Bessie." The Blakes planted the tree several years ago to memorialize Bessie, who had been poisoned by a rival show dog's family. The tree, a rare Japanese weeping spruce, had finally taken root after struggling for several years. At the time of the incident, the tree was five feet tall and flourishing. The tree was worth several thousand dollars and had sentimental value to the Blakes.

The Westons were away for one night visiting their other daughter at her college. They left Alice home alone. Before they left, the Westons asked a neighbor (not the Blakes) to keep an eye on the house and to let them know if they saw any cars or activity going on. They also locked their liquor cabinet. However, there were several six-packs of beer in a basement refrigerator. Because Alice had a test on Monday, they assumed she would have a quiet weekend studying for the test. They did not expect she would have a party and did not hear about the party until the Blakes contacted them.

The minors at the party brought their own beer and also consumed the beer in the Weston's basement.

NY STATUTE

Article 11—OBLIGATIONS TO MAKE COMPENSATION OR RESTITUTION
Title 1—(11-100 - 11-107) COMPENSATION
11-100—Compensation for injury or damage caused by the intoxication of a person under the age of twenty-one years.

Universal Citation: NY Gen. Oblig. L. § 11-100 (2012)

§ 11-100. Compensation for injury or damage caused by the intoxication of a person under the age of twenty-one years.

1. Any person who shall be injured in person, property, means of support or otherwise, by reason of the intoxication or impairment of ability of any person under the age of twenty-one years, whether resulting in his death or not, shall have a right of action to recover actual damages against any person who knowingly causes such intoxication or impairment of ability by unlawfully furnishing to or unlawfully assisting in procuring alcoholic beverages for such person with knowledge or reasonable cause to believe that such person was under the age of twenty-one years.

91 N.Y.2d 355, 693 N.E.2d 1074, 670 N.Y.S.2d 822,
1998 N.Y. Slip Op. 03017

Carol Rust, Appellant,

v.

*Arthur Reyer et al., Defendants, and
Heidi Reyer, Respondent.*

Court of Appeals of New York

Argued February 11, 1998;

Decided April 2, 1998

SUMMARY

Appeal, by permission of the Court of Appeals, from an order of the Appellate Division of the Supreme Court in the Second Judicial Department, entered January 13, 1997, which affirmed so much of an order of the Supreme Court (John S. Lockman, J.), entered in Nassau County, as granted that branch of a motion by defendants Arthur Reyer, Sheila Reyer and Heidi Reyer seeking summary judgment dismissing the second cause of action of the complaint insofar as it was asserted against defendant Heidi Reyer.

Rust v. Reyer, 235 AD2d 413, reversed.

HEADNOTES

Unlawful Furnishing of Alcohol

(1) The host of a "keg party" for minors, who allegedly gave permission to certain persons to provide alcohol at the party she was planning at her house, provided storage for the kegs of beer both before and after the party, negotiated a share of the proceeds from cup sales for herself and at least attempted to arrange for her friends to drink the beer without charge, might be liable as a person who, by "unlawfully furnishing to or unlawfully assisting in procuring alcoholic beverages" for minors, caused the injuries of a third party (General Obligations Law § 11-100 [1]) who was struck by an inebriated party guest during a brawl outside the host's house. If proven at trial, these facts could bring the host's acts within the meaning of "furnishing" as used in the statute. Her role could well be viewed as part of a deliberate plan to provide, supply or give alcohol

to an underage person. The facts alleged demonstrate that she was more than an unknowing bystander or an innocent dupe whose premises were used by other minors seeking to drink, and that she was more than a passive participant who merely knew of the underage drinking and did nothing else to encourage it. She played an indispensable role in the scheme to make the alcohol available to the underage party guests. The purpose of General Obligations Law § 11-100 is to employ civil penalties as a deterrent against underage drinking. Reading the statute to foreclose responsibility in these circumstances would allow unintended circumvention of the legislation and negate its deterrent purpose.

POINTS OF COUNSEL

Carlucci & Legum, L. L. P., Mineola *(Steven G. Legum* of counsel), for appellant.

Since the courts below improperly interpreted the statute, summary judgment dismissing the complaint should not have been granted. Plaintiff has a meritorious claim under General Obligations Law § 11-100. *(People v. Kaplan,* 76 NY2d 140; *People v. Allah,* 71 NY2d 830; *Slocum v. D's & Jayes Val. Rest. & Cafe,* 182 AD2d 981; *Reickert v. Misciagna,* 183 AD2d 151; *Pelinsky v. Rockensies,* 209 AD2d 392; *MacGilvray v. Denino,* 149 AD2d 571; *Graff v. Amodeo,* 178 AD2d 901; *Etu v. Cumberland Farms,* 148 AD2d 821; *Matter of Migliaccio v. O'Connell,* 307 NY 566; *Matter of Cat & Fiddle v. State Liq. Auth.,* 24 AD2d 753.)

Devitt, Spellman, Barrett, Callahan, Leyden & Kenney, L. L. P., Smithtown *(L. Kevin Sheridan* of counsel), for respondent.

On the undisputed facts of this case it should be held that defendant Heidi Reyer cannot be held liable to plaintiff under General Obligations Law § 11-100 (1) for defendant Tarantino's having struck and injured plaintiff. *(Sherman v. Robinson,* 80 NY2d 483; *D'Amico v. Christie,* 71 NY2d 76; *Pelinsky v. Rockensies,* 209 AD2d 392; *Reickert v. Misciagna,* 183 AD2d 151; *MacGilvray v. Denino,* 149 AD2d 571; *Slocum v. D's & Jayes Val. Rest. & Cafe,* 182 AD2d 981; *People v. Keyes,* 75 NY2d 343; *Ball v. Allstate Ins. Co.,* 81 NY2d 22; *Pellicane v. Lambda Chi Alpha Frater-*

nity, 228 AD2d 569; *Aguirre v. City of New York,* 214 AD2d 692.)

OPINION OF THE COURT

Chief Judge KAYE.

This appeal centers on the question whether the host of a "keg party" for minors, in the circumstances presented, might be liable as a person who, by "unlawfully furnishing to or unlawfully assisting in procuring alcoholic beverages" for minors, caused the injuries of a third party (*357 General Obligations Law § 11-100). We conclude that there are material factual issues to be resolved and consequently reverse the Appellate Division order summarily dismissing the second cause of action against defendant Heidi Reyer.

Plaintiff Carol Rust, a minor, was injured when she was punched in the face by Stephen Tarantino, also a minor, after a party at Reyer's house on October 7, 1989. Tarantino had been drinking heavily at the party, and in his inebriated state struck plaintiff during a brawl on the street outside Reyer's house in Merrick, New York.

The facts, viewed in a light most favorable to plaintiff, are as follows. When Reyer, then 17, learned that her parents were going to be on vacation over the weekend of October 7, 1989, she planned a party in their absence. Word of the party reached the ears of a high school fraternity—of which Tarantino was a member—known as the Marquis. Representatives of the fraternity approached Reyer and attempted to convince her to allow them to bring beer. Those attending the party would pay a one-time fee to receive a 16-ounce cup, allowing them unlimited access to the beer. Reyer agreed to have the beer at her party, in exchange for a portion of the proceeds.

On the day of the party, fraternity members arrived with several kegs of beer, which Reyer allowed them to store in the garage. Fraternity members later set up the kegs, where they could be accessed from the Reyers' backyard. As the party started, the fraternity stationed three individuals at the entrance to the backyard, one to collect money, a second to stamp the hands of those who had paid, and a third to hand out cups. Reyer attempted to arrange for her friends to have free beer, and she observed many of the estimated 150 underaged guests consuming alcohol. She did not herself drink or dispense beer at the party, collect money, stamp hands or distribute cups.

Later, responding to neighbors' complaints, the police arrived. Reyer and the police dispersed the party but the guests, including Rust and Tarantino, milled around in the street near Reyer's house. There, a melee erupted and Tarantino—impaired by the alcohol he had consumed at the party—punched plaintiff once in the face, severely injuring her. After the party the kegs were stored in the Reyers' garage, where they were later retrieved by the fraternity. Reyer never received the promised share of the fees, although she sought payment several times after the party. *358

Rust ultimately brought suit against Reyer, her parents and Tarantino, alleging negligence and violations of General Obligations Law §§ 11-100 and 11-101. Tarantino settled with plaintiff, and after joinder of issue the remaining defendants moved for summary judgment on all claims. Plaintiff opposed only that portion of the motion dismissing the General Obligations Law §§ 11-100 claim against Reyer. Supreme Court first dismissed the uncontested claims and then granted the remainder of defendant's motion. Relying on the principle that statutes in derogation of the common law are to be narrowly construed, the court held that while "Heidi Reyer may be said to have 'facilitated' the furnishing of beer to Stephen Tarantino and other party guests, the statute cannot be stretched to impose liability for this type of conduct." The court further concluded that Reyer had not assisted in procuring the alcohol, because fraternity members had purchased the beer, brought it to the party and personally dispensed it.

Plaintiff appealed only that portion of Supreme Court's order dismissing the General Obligations Law §§ 11-100 claim against Reyer, and the Appellate Division affirmed. That court held that "General Obligations Law §§ 11-100 is not applicable to a homeowner who has neither supplied alcohol to nor procured alcohol for consumption by an underage person" 235 AD2d 413). We granted plaintiff leave to appeal and now reverse.

Analysis

Underage drinking is a significant societal problem that has generated widespread concern (*see, e.g.,* French, Kaput and Wildman, *Special Project: Social Host Liability for the Negligent Acts of Intoxicated Guests,* 70 Cornell L Rev 1058 [1985]; Comment, *Killer Party: Proposing Civil Liability for Social Hosts who Serve Alcohol to Minors,* 30 J Marshall L Rev 245, 257-258 [1996] ["*Killer Party*"]). All 50 States have set minimum drinking ages, a measure which has to some extent prevented minors from themselves purchasing alcohol at bars and liquor stores.[1] Those same laws, however, have proven far less effective in stopping minors from obtaining alcohol in a social setting, where it is provided to them by individuals who have little, if any, financial disincentive for doing so (*see, e.g., Killer Party, op. cit.,* at 260).

States have responded to this circumvention of their minimum age laws in a variety of ways. Some have by statute *359 imposed civil liability, criminal liability or both on gratuitous providers of alcohol. In other States, courts have recognized a common-law duty of the provider (*see generally,* Annotation, *Social Host's Liability For Injuries Incurred By Third Parties As A Result Of Intoxicated Guest's Negligence,* 62 ALR4th 16). New York has taken the former approach: in addition to making it a crime to furnish alcoholic beverages to a minor in most cases (Penal Law § 260.20 [2]), in 1983 the Legislature enacted General Obligations Law §§ 11-100, which provides:

"Any person who shall be injured in person, property, means of support or otherwise, by reason of the intoxication or impairment of ability of any person under the age of twenty-one years, whether resulting in his death or not, shall have a right of action to recover actual damages against any person who *knowingly causes such intoxication or impairment of ability by unlawfully furnishing to or unlawfully assisting in procuring alcoholic beverages* for such person with knowledge or reasonable cause to believe that such person was under the age of twenty-one years" (General Obligations Law §§ 11-100 [1] [emphasis supplied]).[2]

Conceding that Reyer herself never actually served alcohol to any party guest, plaintiff nonetheless contends that Reyer's actions constituted "furnishing" under the statute. Neither the relevant statutes (including related enactments General Obligations Law §§ 11-101 and Alcoholic Beverage Control Law § 65) nor our prior cases define the term "furnishing," which is ordinarily understood to mean "to provide in any way," "to supply" or "to give" (*see, e.g.,* Black's Law Dictionary 675 [6th ed 1990]; Webster's Deluxe Unabridged Dictionary 743 [2d ed 1983]; *accord, Ball v. Allstate Ins. Co.,* 81 NY2d 22, 25).

Here, Reyer allegedly gave permission for the alcohol at the party she was planning, provided storage for the kegs of beer both before and after the party, negotiated a share of·the proceeds from cup sales for herself and at least attempted to arrange for her friends to drink the beer without charge. Her request for a portion of the proceeds from cup sales underscores her complete complicity in the fraternity's plans to furnish beer. As stated in plaintiff's affidavit, Reyer "chose to participate *360 in a scheme to furnish alcohol to underage individuals in return for a payment of money." Moreover, without Reyer's advance permission, the beer could not have been served as it ultimately was. Indeed, many of the 150 minors present may well not have come to the party in the first instance had they not known that alcohol would be available.

We conclude that if proven at trial, these facts could bring Reyer's acts within the meaning of "furnishing" as used in the statute.[3] Reyer's role could well be viewed as part of a deliberate plan to provide, supply or give alcohol to an underage person.

In reaching this conclusion we are mindful that a statute in derogation of the common law must be strictly construed (*see, Sherman v. Robinson,* 80 NY2d 483, 487; *D'Amico v. Christie,* 71 NY2d 76, 83). We are mindful as well that our prime directive, in matters of statutory interpretation, is to give effect to the intention of the Legislature (*see, Ferres v. City of New Rochelle,* 68 NY2d 446, 451; *People v. Ryan,* 274 NY 149, 152). To interpret "furnishing" as Reyer suggests—in effect limiting it to those who hand the alcohol to the minor—gives the term an overly narrow reach that undermines the clear legislative goal.

The purpose of General Obligations Law §§ 11-100 is to employ civil penalties as a deterrent against underage drinking (*Sheehy v. Big Flats Community Day,* 73 NY2d 629, 636). As the bill's cosponsor noted, "[t]his legislation seeks to protect minors from those persons uncaring enough to provide intoxicating beverages to minors in an indiscriminate manner and by so doing, to endanger the life and safety of the minor as well as of the general public" (Letter of Assemblymember John F. Duane, Bill Jacket, L 1983, ch 641). In the words of Senator William T. Smith, also a cosponsor of the statute:

"Over the years, numerous court cases have dealt extensively with the question of common law liability on the part of those who knowingly furnish alcoholic beverages to under-age persons at graduation parties, church socials, wedding receptions, office parties, and college campuses. Under-age persons consuming excess alcohol at these social events unquestionably have the same propensity to do harm to the traveling public as those who have *361 been served alcohol pursuant to a sale" (1983 NY Legis Ann, at 281).

The facts alleged demonstrate that Reyer was more than an unknowing bystander or an innocent dupe whose premises were used by other minors seeking to drink (*cf., Dodge v. Victory Mkts.,* 199 AD2d 917; *Reickert v. Misciagna,* 183 AD2d 151). Similarly, she was more than a passive participant who merely knew of the underage drinking and did nothing else to encourage it (*cf., Lane v. Barker,* 241 AD2d 739; *MacGilvray v. Denino,* 149 AD2d 571; *see also, Pelinsky v. Rockensies,* 209 AD2d 392). Reyer played an indispensable role in the scheme to make the alcohol available to the underage party guests.

Reading the statute to foreclose responsibility in these circumstances would allow unintended circumvention of the legislation and negate its deterrent purpose (*see,* 1983 NY Legis Ann, at 281-282 [the "time has come for every individual to accept responsibility for an activity which most people partake in, consumption of alcoholic beverages—the responsibility as a consumer, and as a furnisher, as well"]; *see also, Killer Party, op. cit.,* at 249-250).

Accordingly, the order of the Appellate Division should be reversed, with costs, and the motion for summary judgment dismissing the second cause of action against defendant Heidi Reyer should be denied.

Judges Titone, Bellacosa, Smith, Levine, Ciparick and Wesley concur.

Order reversed, etc. *362

Copr. (c) 2014, Secretary of State, State of New York

Footnotes

1

Alocholic Beverage Control Law § 65 establishes 21 as the minimum drinking age in New York.

2

The statute was amended in 1985 to match the Legislature's decision to raise the minimum drinking age in this State from 19 to 21 (*see,* L 1985, ch 274, § 4).

3

Given this conclusion, we need not and do not reach plaintiff's alternative contention that defendant "unlawfully assist[ed] in procuring" alcohol for an underage person.

183 A.D.2d 151, 590 N.Y.S.2d 100

Jeffrey Reickert, Plaintiff, and Marilyn Reickert, Appellant,

v.

Pasquale Misciagna et al., Respondents.

Supreme Court, Appellate Division, Second Department, New York

November 2, 1992

CITE TITLE AS: Reickert v Misciagna

SUMMARY

Appeal from so much of a judgment of the Supreme Court (John DiNoto, J.), entered May 22, 1990 in Nassau County, as, upon granting defendants' separate motions for summary judgment, dismissed the remaining cause of action asserted in the complaint.

HEADNOTES

Intoxicating Liquors

Liability of Social Host

Failure to Supervise Underage Persons

([1]) A parent cannot be held liable pursuant to General Obligations Law § 11-100, which imposes liability for injuries caused by intoxicated individuals who have not reached the legal drinking age upon persons "unlawfully furnishing" alcoholic beverages to them, where the parent does not actually furnish or assist in procuring alcoholic beverages to persons under the legal drinking age, but allegedly contributes to an atmosphere where alcoholic beverages were available by failing to supervise underage persons who were present in his or her residence, albeit without the parents' knowledge or permission. Accordingly, where the then 18-year-old plaintiff consumed large amounts of alcoholic beverages at the residence of defendants, who were not present and did not have knowledge that plaintiff was drinking in their home, and then dove into a swimming pool at the residence of other defendants, without their

knowledge or permission, sustaining injuries that left him permanently paralyzed, Supreme Court properly dismissed plaintiff's mother's cause of action asserted pursuant to General Obligations Law § 11-100. The statute was not intended to impose liability for underage drinking which occurs upon an individual's premises without his or her knowledge or permission, or with alcoholic beverages over which he or she has no control.

Intoxicating Liquors

Liability of Social Host

Failure to Supervise Underage Persons—Damages

([2]) In an action to recover damages for injuries sustained by the then 18-year-old plaintiff when, after consuming large amounts of alcoholic beverages at the residence of defendants, who were not present and had no knowledge that plaintiff was drinking in their home, he dove into a swimming pool at other defendants' residence, without their knowledge or permission, appellant, plaintiff's mother, may not assert a claim for damages pursuant to General Obligations Law § 11-100 (4). While that provision states "[i]n any case where parents shall be entitled to [actual] damages, either of such parents may bring an action therefor" and thus does not depend upon the pendency of a cause of action on behalf of the injured person, section 11-100 (4) must be read in conjunction with General Obligations Law § 11-100 (1), which imposes liability for injuries caused by intoxicated individuals who have not reached the legal drinking age upon persons "unlawfully furnishing" alcoholic beverages to them; General Obligations *152 Law § 11-100 (4) will only give rise to a cause of action in favor of parents where it can be shown that a defendant furnished or assisted in procuring alcoholic beverages for the parent's child. Here, the injured plaintiff's intoxicated state was induced by alcohol which he himself procured and not as a result of alcoholic beverages furnished by defendants; defendants are not, accordingly, liable to appellant on her derivative claim for medical expenses.

Negligence

Duty

Liability for Injury Sustained by Intoxicated Minor

([3]) In an action to recover damages for injuries sustained by the then 18-year-old plaintiff when, after consuming large amounts of alcoholic beverages at the residence of defendants, who were not present and had no knowledge that plaintiff was drinking in their home, he dove into a swimming pool at other defendants' residence, without their knowledge or permission, common-law claims asserted by appellant, plaintiff's mother, against defendants did not survive the settlement of plaintiff's action against defendants, as none of the defendants had the opportunity to control the injured plaintiff and the other underage drinkers who were present, nor were they reasonably aware of the need for such control.

TOTAL CLIENT SERVICE LIBRARY REFERENCES

Am Jur 2d, Intoxicating Liquors, § 553.

General Obligations Law §11-100.

NY Jur 2d, Alcoholic Beverages, §125.5; Negligence, §15.

ANNOTATION REFERENCES

Liability of persons furnishing intoxicating liquor for injury to or death of consumer, outside coverage of civil damages acts. 98 ALR3d 1230.

APPEARANCES OF COUNSEL

Meiselman, Boland, Reilly & Fugazzi, Mineola (*Donald J. Boland* and *John Reilly* of counsel), for appellant.

Curtis, Zaklukiewicz, Vasile, Devine & McElhenny, Merrick (*John P. Humphreys* of counsel), for Pasquale Misciagna and another, respondents.

John P. Coogan, Wantagh, for Ray Forkel, Sr., and another, respondents.

OPINION OF THE COURT

Santucci, J.

The question presented on this appeal is whether, as a matter of law, a parent can be held liable pursuant to *153 General Obligations Law § 11-100 where the parent does not actually furnish or assist in procuring alcoholic beverages to persons under the legal drinking age, but allegedly contributes to an atmosphere where alcoholic beverages were available by failing to supervise underage persons who were present in his or her residence, albeit without the parents' knowledge or permission.

On July 21, 1985, the plaintiff Jeffrey Reickert, then aged 18, spent several hours at the residence of the defendants Forkel. During that time Jeffrey, the Forkel's son, and some other friends consumed large amounts of alcoholic beverages. The defendants Ray Forkel, Sr., and Didi Forkel were not present at their home during this time, nor did they have any knowledge that Jeffrey and the others were drinking in their home. Later that same day the daughter of the defendants Misciagna invited Jeffrey, among others, over for a barbeque and swim at her parents' home, also without her parents' knowledge or permission. Soon after his arrival at the Misciagna residence, and without having consumed any alcoholic beverages on the Misciagna's property, Jeffrey dove into the Misciagna's above-ground pool. Jeffrey hit his head on the bottom of the pool rendering him unconscious and, ultimately, permanently paralyzed.

In September 1987, the plaintiffs, Jeffrey Reickert and his mother Marilyn Reickert, commenced an action against the defendants Misciagna and Forkel. The action between the plaintiff Jeffrey Reickert and the defendants was subsequently settled. On or about November 14, 1989, the defendants Misciagna and Forkel moved separately pursuant to General Obligations Law § 11-100 for summary judgment dismissing the remaining cause of action asserted by Marilyn Reickert. Marilyn Reickert's other causes of action were previously dismissed and are not the subject of this appeal.

([1]) By order dated March 19, 1990, the Supreme Court, Nassau County (DiNoto, J.), granted the defendants' motions for summary judgment dismissing the complaint and all cross claims. With respect to the defendants Forkel, the court found that those defendants "did...not procure for or furnish to Jeffrey Reickert any of the alcoholic beverages which he admittedly consumed". With respect to the defendants Misciagna, the court found that they too "did not give, offer or furnish any alcohol to the...plaintiff or anyone else at [their] home on [that] day". Accordingly, the court held: "In the absence of any factual evidence to rebut that offered by *154 defendants and by plaintiff's son, himself, with regard to defendants' conduct in the light of General Obligations Law § 11-100, summary judgment in their favor is clearly warranted". For the reasons stated below we affirm.

Under common law, the provider of intoxicating liquor was not held liable for injuries caused by the drinker, as "it was the drinking of the alcohol, not the furnishing of it, that was regarded as the proximate cause of alcohol-induced injury" (*D'Amico v. Christie*, 71 NY2d 76, 84-85). However, General Obligations Law § 11-101 (the Dram Shop Act) created a cause of action against one who unlawfully *sells* alcoholic beverages to an intoxicated person on behalf of a person who has sustained injury caused by the intoxicated person (*see, Delamater v. Kimmerle*, 104 AD2d 242, 244). As an exception to the common-law rule, General Obligations Law § 11-101 is to be narrowly construed (*see, D'Amico v. Christie, supra*, at 83; *Delamater v. Kimmerle, supra*, at 244).

In 1983, the Legislature enacted General Obligations Law § 11-100, which, "in contrast to the Dram Shop Act, impose[d] liability for injuries caused by intoxicated individuals who have not reached the legal drinking age upon persons 'unlawfully furnishing' alcoholic beverages to them" (*D'Amico v. Christie, supra*, at 84). Specifically, General Obligations Law § 11-100 states in relevant part, as follows: "Any person who shall be injured in person, property, means of support or otherwise, by reason of the intoxication or impairment of ability of any person under the age of twenty-one years, whether resulting in his death or not, shall have a right of action to recover actual damages against any person who *knowingly causes such intoxication or impairment of ability by unlawfully furnishing to or unlawfully assisting in procuring alcoholic beverages for such person with knowledge or reasonable cause to believe that such person was under the age of twenty-one years*" (emphasis supplied).*

The legislative memorandum in support of General Obligations Law § 11-100 (1983 NY Legis Ann, at 281-282) provides insight into the purpose of the statute. In comparing General Obligations Law § 11-101 (the Dram Shop Act) with proposed General Obligations Law § 11-100, Senator Smith noted, as *155 follows: "To place upon those *wishing to furnish* alcoholic beverages without charge a duty to know or have reason to know the age of the person being served and the apparent condition of the person so served does not place an inconceivable burden.... To *voluntarily provide* alcoholic beverages to an under-age person who is already intoxicated is morally irresponsible behavior and cannot be condoned. The time has come for every individual to accept responsibility for an activity which most people partake in, consumption of alcoholic beverages—the responsibility as a consumer, and as a furnisher, as well" *(ibid.;* emphasis supplied).

The crux of appellant's argument is that a parent can be held liable under General Obligations Law § 11-100 if he or she "constructively" furnishes or assists in procuring alcoholic beverages to underage persons by, specifically, failing to supervise such individuals at his or her residence. In the case at bar, the record reveals that the liquor consumed by the plaintiff Jeffrey Reickert took place only at the Forkel residence when the adult Forkels were not present. There is no evidence that the Forkels had any knowledge of, or that they had given any permission for, the consumption of alcoholic beverages by their son and his underage friends during their absence. Moreover, the alcohol which was consumed at the Forkel residence was mainly beer, which had been procured elsewhere and brought into the Forkel home on the day of the accident. Indeed, the injured plaintiff supplied himself with the two "eight packs" of beer which he consumed at the Forkel residence. The record also reveals that the injured plaintiff and his friends drank some "korn liquor" which had been previously obtained in Georgia by the Forkel's son without the knowledge of his parents. With respect to the Misciagnas, the injured plaintiff himself stated that he did not consume any alcoholic beverages while at the Misciagna house.

Under these circumstances, and in view of the legislative history, it is clear that General Obligations Law § 11-100 was not intended to impose liability for underage drinking which occurs upon an individual's premises without his or her knowledge or permission, or with alcoholic beverages over which he or she has no control. It was the intent of the Legislature that the furnisher or procurer of alcoholic beverages be actually aware of their actions, as Senator Smith's memorandum specifically notes that the "voluntary" furnishing, and not the negligent furnishing of alcohol to persons underage, is "morally irresponsible" (*see also, MacGilvray v.* ***156** *Denino,* 149 AD2d 571). Moreover, because it is in derogation of the common law, General Obligations Law § 11-100 is to be narrowly construed and should not be accorded the expansive interpretation which the appellant urges herein (*see,* McKinney's Cons Laws of NY, Book 1, Statutes § 301; *MacGilvray v. Denino, supra,* at 572; *Delamater v. Kimmerle,* 104 AD2d 242, 244, *supra).*

([2]) We also conclude that, under the circumstances of this case, the appellant may not assert a claim for damages pursuant to General Obligations Law § 11-100 (4). That provision states, in pertinent part, "[i]n any case where parents shall be entitled to [actual] damages, either of such parents may bring an action therefor". It is true that a cause of action pursuant to this section is entirely statutory and, therefore, does not depend upon the pendency of a cause of action on behalf of the injured person (*see, Wilkins v. Weresiuk,* 64 Misc 2d 736, 738-739). However, this section must be read in conjunction with General Obligations Law § 11-100 (1) which states that: "Any person who shall be injured... by reason of the intoxication...of any person under the age of twenty-one years...shall have a right of action to recover...damages against any person who knowingly causes such intoxication...by unlawfully furnishing to or unlawfully assisting in procuring alcoholic beverages for such person". Thus, General Obligations Law § 11-100 (4) will only give rise to a cause of action in favor of parents where it can be shown that a defendant furnished to or assisted in procuring alcoholic beverages for the parent's child. In the case at bar, the injured plaintiff's intoxicated state was induced by alcohol which he himself procured and not as a result of alcoholic beverages furnished by the defendants. Under these circumstances, the defendants are not liable to the plaintiff's mother on her derivative claim for medical expenses (*cf., Reuter v. Flobo Enters.,* 120 AD2d 722). This is so even though appellant has a duty to support her son until he reaches 21 years of age (*see, Vandenburg v. Brosnan,* 129 AD2d 793, 794; *Van Neil v. Hopper,* 167 AD2d 954; *cf., Comeau v. Lucas,* 90 AD2d 674, 674-675).

([3]) Furthermore, we find that the appellant's common-law claims against the defendants did not survive the settlement of her son's action, as none of the defendants had the "opportunity to control" the injured plaintiff and the other underage drinkers, nor were they "reasonably aware of the need for such control" (*D'Amico v. Christie,* 71 NY2d 76, *supra,* at 85). ***157**

The appellant's remaining contention regarding the adequacy of discovery is unpreserved for appellate review and, in any event, is without merit (*see, Adelman v. Island Holding Corp.,* 157 AD2d 637).

Accordingly, the judgment is affirmed insofar as appealed from.

Mangano, P. J., Harwood and Miller, JJ., concur.

Ordered that the judgment is affirmed insofar as appealed from, with one bill of costs to the respondents appearing separately and filing separate briefs. *158

Copr. (c) 2015, Secretary of State, State of New York

Footnotes

* At the time this statute was enacted the legal drinking age in New York was 19. Thereafter, on December 1, 1985, it was changed to 21 (General Obligations Law § 11-100, as amended by L 1985, ch 274, § 4). At the time of the accident on July 1, 1985, the plaintiff Jeffrey Reickert was 18 years old and the legal drinking age was 19.

274 A.D.2d 553, 712 N.Y.S.2d 143,
2000 N.Y. Slip Op. 07207

Carlo Guercia, Respondent,
v.
Steven Carter, Defendant, Brad Lopez, Respondent,
and Philip Bellini et al., Appellants.

Supreme Court, Appellate Division,
Second Department, New York

(July 31, 2000)

In an action to recover damages for personal injuries, the defendants Philip Bellini, Michael Bellini, and Loretta Bellini appeal from an order of the Supreme Court, Nassau County (DiNoto, J.), dated July 8, 1999, which denied their motion for summary judgment dismissing the complaint and all cross claims insofar as asserted against them.

Ordered that the order is reversed, on the law, with costs, the motion is granted, the complaint and all cross claims are dismissed insofar as asserted against the appellants, and the action against the remaining defendants is severed.

The plaintiff commenced this action after he was allegedly *554 assaulted by the defendants Steven Carter and Brad Lopez while attending a party hosted by the then 16-year-old defendant Philip Bellini. The gathering took place at the Syosset home of Philip's parents, the defendants Michael Bellini and Loretta Bellini (hereinafter the Bellinis), while the Bellinis were out of town for the weekend. Before going away, the Bellinis had given their permission for Philip to invite a few "close friends" over to the house in their absence. The Bellinis had also requested that their adult daughter, who no longer lived in Syosset, return home for the weekend in question, which she did. The plaintiff alleges that he was injured as a result of the intoxication of individuals under 21 years of age, who were furnished liquor at the party, and because the Bellinis failed to properly exercise control and supervision over their premises.

There is no evidence that the Bellinis were aware of, or that they had given permission for, the consumption of alcoholic beverages on their premises by underage people. There is also no evidence that Phillip Bellini furnished or procured alcoholic beverages for any of the people who attended his gathering. Moreover, there is no proof that either Carter or Lopez was intoxicated at the time of the alleged assault. Under these circumstances, the Bellini defendants established their prima facie entitlement to summary judgment dismissing the complaint insofar as it was based upon General Obligations Law § 11-100 or upon a violation of Alcoholic Beverage Control Law § 65 (*see, Reickert v. Misciagna,* 183 AD2d 151; *cf., Rust v. Reyer,* 235 AD2d 413, revd 91 NY2d 355). The plaintiff's conclusory speculation to the contrary is insufficient to defeat the motion (*see, Alvarez v. Prospect Hosp.,* 68 NY2d 320, 324).

The plaintiff also failed to demonstrate a cause of action predicated upon common-law negligence since there was no evidence that the Bellini defendants had the opportunity to control the conduct of either Lopez or Carter, or that they were aware of the need to do so. Such elements are "prerequisites to imposing [common-law] liability upon a landowner" in this type of situation (*Demarest v. Bailey,* 246 AD2d 772, 773).

Accordingly, the Bellini defendants are entitled to summary judgment.

Bracken, J. P., Santucci, McGinity and Feuerstein, JJ., concur.

A. ADDRESSING THE CLIENT'S PROBLEM

As we know, a legal analysis begins with a client's problem. Most clients, whether they are individuals, businesses, organizations, or government entities, will come to you with a story and a set of facts, and ask for your expert advice or information about how to proceed. The steps you take to help your client will naturally vary depending on the particular situation but will generally follow these steps:

1. Understand the facts of your client's case.
2. Identify the area of law that is likely to hold the answer to the legal issue in the case (e.g., employment law, medical malpractice law, criminal law).
3. Research the law. This might start with reading a treatise or other secondary source.
4. Read and study relevant statutes and cases.
5. Identify the key facts from case law or legal principles that apply to your client's problem.
6. Review your client's facts and identify the key, decisive facts.
7. Narrow the body of legal authority that addresses your client's problem, winnowing out authority that is not on point.
8. Outline the legal analysis.
9. Begin the writing process. Once you are ready to write, you will embark on another multi-step process required to complete a legal analysis. We will cover these later.

B. READING AND UNDERSTANDING A STATUTE

In the Weston facts, you learned that the clients' neighbors have threatened to sue them under a New York statute. You will learn how to find a statute in your legal research class. Once you have found it, you will have to study it and identify what the statute actually prohibits.

Recall that statutes come from the legislative branch of government. What is contained in a statute is law. Statutory law (from the legislature) or regulatory law (from agencies) can govern criminal conduct and civil conduct.

Although case file 1 does not require you to examine a regulation, it is helpful to remember that in any given legal problem, your research may lead you to a statute, which in turn leads you to a regulation. Regulatory rules are enacted by agencies to carry out laws enacted by the legislature (either state or federal). Remember the woman who believes she was fired because of her age? The employer's conduct would be regulated by federal or state statutes or regulations that govern civil behavior.

The legislature or the agencies do not necessarily have the last word on what the law is as it is applied to individuals or businesses. The United

States operates under a common law system and thus it is up to the courts to interpret statutes and regulations once litigants raise questions about them.

Litigants can challenge statutes for a variety of reasons, including on the basis of consitutionality. Litigants can also take issue with words or phrases in a statute that are arguably ambiguous. This type of claim usually occurs when a litigant believes that the statute has been applied to his or her situation incorrectly or illegally.

Thus, challenges to statutes do not arise in a vacuum; they arise because the statute has been applied to litigants in a way that they believe is unlawful. A particular law may apply to a multitude of factual situations. Consider the New York "social host" statute. That statute prohibits "furnishing" alcohol to an underage person. Can the statute apply even though the Westons were away and not aware that their daughter was having a party? To answer this, you have to study how the legislature defines "furnish." Then you have to study how the courts have applied the legislature's definition of "furnish."

Let's take a close look at the statute that will decide the Westons' fate:

McKinney's Consolidated Laws of New York Annotated
 General Obligation Law (Refs & Annos)
  Chapter 24-A. Of the Consolidated Laws (Refs & Annos)

   McKinney's General Obligations Law § 11-100

§ 11-100. Compensation for injury or damage caused by the intoxication of a person under the age of twenty-one years.

1. Any person who shall be injured in person, property, means of support or otherwise, by reason of the intoxication or impairment of ability of any person under the age of twenty-one years, whether resulting in his death or not, shall have a right of action to recover actual damages against any person who knowingly causes such intoxication or impairment of ability by unlawfully furnishing to or unlawfully assisting in procuring alcoholic beverages for such person with knowledge or reasonable cause to believe that such person was under the age of twenty-one years.

2. In case of the death of either party, the action or right of action established by the provisions of this section shall survive to or against his or her executor or administrator, and the amount so recovered by either a husband, wife or child shall be his or her sole and separate property.

3. Such action may be brought in any court of competent jurisdiction.

4. In any case where parents shall be entitled to such damages, either of such parents may bring an action therefor; but that recovery by either one of such parties shall constitute a bar to suit brought by the other.

Credits
(Added L.1983, c. 641, § 1. Amended L.1985, c. 274, § 4.)

This is how New York Laws are codified

The statutes are divided into Chapters and Sections

This is the specific name of the "Social Host Law"

Note that the statute prohibits two types of conduct: (1) "furnishing to" and (2) "assisting in procuring." The statute applies if an individual has either direct "knowledge" or "cause to believe" that the person is a minor.

When there is an injury to a third party caused by an intoxicated minor, individuals are liable under the Social Host law for knowingly causing a minor's intoxication, either by unlawfully furnishing or unlawfully assisting in procuring alcoholic beverages for a minor when they have actual knowledge or a reasonable belief that the individual is under 21.

Most statutes can be deconstructed into specific elements. One way to think about elements is to ask: "What must the plaintiff (or state in a criminal case) prove?" Here the statute requires that certain elements must be met, although there are alternative ways to meet them. This formulation—requiring a number of elements be met—is called **conjunctive** (usually indicated by "and"). Where there are alternative ways to meet a statute, the formulation is called **disjunctive** (indicated by "or"). The New York statute in case file 1 is a good example of a law that incorporates both. Although the word "and" doesn't appear in the statute, liability exists only when a person knowingly causes intoxication *and* when that person knows or has reason to know the intoxicated individual is under 21. Often the conjunctive elements in a statute are implicit. Studying and breaking down the statute will reveal which parts are conjunctive.

Breaking down a statute and identifying its elements is essential to legal analysis and such a key aspect of a lawyer's job that it's worth looking at some other illustrations before returning to our underage drinking party. First let's examine the following Maine statute that prohibits distracted driving. Look for italicized words that signal conjunction and disjunction.

> **Failure to maintain control of a motor vehicle.** A person commits the traffic infraction of failure to maintain control of a motor vehicle if the person:
>
> **A.** Commits either a traffic infraction under this Title *or* commits the crime of driving to endanger under section 2413 *and*, at the time the traffic infraction or crime occurred, the person was engaged in the operation of a motor vehicle while distracted; *or*
>
> **B.** Is determined to have been the operator of a motor vehicle that was involved in a reportable accident as defined in section 2251, subsection 1 that resulted in property damage *and*, at the time the reportable accident occurred, the person was engaged in the operation of a motor vehicle while distracted.

Recall from Chapter 3 that legislatures can sometimes make it difficult to identify the elements that make up a statutory violation. It would be useful if every statute looked like this:

> Violating the Burglary Statute requires the following elements:
> • breaking and entering
> • into a dwelling
> • with the intent to commit a misdemeanor therein

Unfortunately, many statutes do not break down the elements so clearly, and thus we are left to dissect the statute and figure out what elements make up a violation or a cause of action.

Let's do this by examining New Jersey's "dog bite" statute. Imagine that your client, a 16-year-old girl, was bitten by a dog after she let herself into her friend's house to retrieve her iPod that she had left there by accident. She had let herself into the house many times in the past, as she knew where the family kept a hidden key. The family was aware that she had done this and never objected. However, on this occasion she startled the dog, and he bit her in the leg, causing a deep cut.

Here is what the New Jersey Dog Bite Statute says:

> The owner of any dog which shall bite a person while such person is on or in a public place, or lawfully on or in a private place including the property of the owner of the dog, shall be liable for such damages as may be suffered by the person bitten, regardless of the former viciousness of such dog or the owner's knowledge of such viciousness.

Your first step is to identify what you must show in order to make a viable complaint against the family. To be viable, you would have to show that all requirements of the statute have been met. So let's break it down:

The owner of any dog—[*tells you who can violate the statute*]

which shall bite a person—[*tells you what act the statute prohibits*]

while such person is on or in a public place or lawfully on or in a private place, including the property of the owner of the dog,—[*tells you the circumstances that must be present for a violation of the statute*]

shall be liable for such damages as may be suffered by the person bitten—[*tells you that the owner* will *be liable, which means that this is a strict liability statute; the state of mind of the owner does not matter*]

regardless of the former viciousness of the dog or the owner's knowledge of such viciousness.—[*tells you that the dog owner has no defense to the violation if he or she was unaware of the dog's propensity to violence*]

The basic requirements, or elements, are that:

- The defendant is the owner of the dog.
- The dog bit the plaintiff.
- The bite happened when the plaintiff was in or on a public place or lawfully in or on a private place.

Very often a court will have already gone through this process and identified the elements of a statute. Once you know what statute or statutes you are dealing with, the next step is to see if the courts have addressed the elements of the statute. For example, if the above set of facts had occurred in New Jersey, you could have researched the Dog Bite Statute and discovered this case:

Devito v. Anderson, 410 N.J. Super. 175, 980 A.2d 498 (2009)

[Excerpted]

Plaintiffs Sandra DeVivo and John DeVivo ("DeVivos") bring this motion before the court seeking summary judgment as to liability against defendants Britney Anderson and Suzanne Anderson ("Andersons"). Plaintiffs allege that the Andersons are strictly liable pursuant to N.J.S.A. 4:19-16, the so called "dog bite" statute, for Sandra DeVivo's injuries. Sandra contends that Suzanne Anderson's German Shepherd dog, Magic, bit her on the forearm as she was walking past the front of defendants' residence. At the time Magic was unleashed. Britney, Suzanne's daughter, was holding on to Magic by his collar. Also before the court is defendants' cross-motion for summary judgment. Defendants contend that Sandra cannot meet the statutory requirements of N.J.S.A. 4:19-16 since "there was no broken skin or evidence of any type of bite caused..." by Magic. Defendants' notice of motion also seeks summary judgment with respect to plaintiffs' common law negligence cause of action.

...*N.J.S.A.* 4:19-16 imposes strict liability upon an owner whose dog bites another, without proof of the owner's knowledge of the dog's vicious propensities. The "dog bite" statute states:

> The owner of any dog which shall bite a person while such person is on or in a public place, or lawfully on or in a private place including the property of the owner of the dog, shall be liable for such damages as may be suffered by the person bitten, regardless of the former viciousness of such dog or the owner's knowledge of such viciousness.

Thus, "[t]he three elements plaintiff must prove under N.J.S.A. 4:19-16 are that: (1) defendant is the owner of the dog; (2) the dog bit plaintiff; and (3) the bite occurred while the plaintiff was either in a public place or lawfully in a private place." *Trisuzzi v. Tabatchnik*, 285 N.J. Super. 15, 23, 666 A.2d 543 (App. Div.1995).

In the instant matter, there is no dispute as to the first and third elements. Defendant, Suzanne Anderson, admits that she is Magic's owner and that plaintiff, Sandra DeVivo, was in a public place when the incident occurred. With respect to the second element, the parties dispute whether a "dog bite" occurred sufficient to meet the requirements of N.J.S.A. 4:19-16. Defendants argue that no bite occurred because, based on the hospital reports, there was no broken skin or any evidence of any type of a bite. Defendants point to the assessment/treatment notes in Sandra's hospital records which state "right arm swelling noted. Skin intact. No broken/open areas noted." Defendants further contend that there is no evidence as to the cause of the bruising on Sandra's arm and deny that the photographs of Sandra's injuries depict bruising on her right arm resulting from Magic's teeth. Defendants conceded at oral argument that there may be circumstances in which a "bite" may occur despite the fact that no tearing of the skin occurred. However, under these circumstances, defendants argue Sandra was not bitten by Magic.

The court tells you what the elements are. Here, the issue centers on the "bite" element, but not what it means to be lawfully on another's property. For our client, we would have to research cases that discuss this particular element to find out if our client has a viable clam.

> **PRACTICAL TIP**
>
> Model jury instructions are a good resource for analyzing statutes. Many states have model jury instructions, which are templates that judges use when instructing a jury about what they must find in a particular case. Jury instructions are usually written by a committee of state bar members and judges, and the instructions typically outline the elements of a crime (in a criminal case) or cause of action (in a civil case). They are usually available online or through the state's bar association.

This dog bite case also illustrates the importance of definitions. In this instance the definition of what represents a "bite" is potentially at issue. In our drinking party case, "knowingly" and "furnishing" will need further definition. Many statutes include a definitional section. Usually this appears at the beginning of a particular title or chapter, or it can appear at the beginning of the entire statutory code. Part of understanding a statute includes checking if particular words or phrases have been defined by the legislature in the appropriate definitional section. Even when terms are defined in a statute, courts often interpret, elucidate, or alter those definitions. Whether terms are defined or not, it is typically necessary to research how courts have applied those terms.

C. HOW DO COURTS INTERPRET STATUTES?

A significant amount of a lawyer's time is spent analyzing a court's interpretation of a statute. Courts follow some basic rules when they interpret and apply statutes. These are known as the Canons of Construction. Here is a brief description of the most widely used rules:

- *Plain Meaning Rule.* The court will look at the actual words of the statute and apply a common, ordinary meaning. Sometimes a court will use a dictionary definition of a common word to identify its meaning.
- *Legislative Intent.* The court will examine documents (e.g., hearing minutes, committee reports, or preambles) to discern what the legislators' goals were in drafting the statute. Sometimes a court will examine other parts of a statute, or the statute as a whole, to discover the legislative intent.
- *Stare Decisis.* The court may examine other courts' interpretations of the statute.

After you have a good understanding of the statute, the next step is to examine whether the statute is a good fit given your client's facts. What questions do you have about how the statute might apply? This inquiry will likely point you toward case law, and thus the next step is to read cases where the court has applied the statute's terms. In the case of the Westons, we are interested in the term "furnish."

CASE FILE 1: On Your Own—Understanding a Statute

1. Study the New York statute. Outline the elements that are required for liability under the statute.

D. BRIEFING CASES AND CLOSE CASE READING

1. Briefing a Case

Careful case reading and effective case briefing are skills you will use throughout your career. At first, your case briefs will follow a format suggested to you. As you progress through law school and in your legal employment, you will adapt your briefing format to a style that works for you. You may find that the way you brief a case for your classes is different than how you brief cases you read for a research project. What follows is a suggested format. At first, briefing a case will take you a long time. As you get used to it, the process will go faster, but don't try to rush through. Careful reading and analysis is at the very core of good lawyering.

a. Why Brief Cases?
- Because briefing forces you to study the case to understand and condense its most important information.
- Because briefing helps you organize the cases. This is especially true when your research project involves numerous cases.
- Because briefing helps you to efficiently refer to cases as you are writing your memorandum.

b. General Tips on Briefing
- Study cases you read for a research project in the same way you study a case to prepare for a class. Re-read the case several times, highlighting and taking notes about what you are reading.
- Remember that the headnotes at the beginning of an opinion are not part of the opinion and are not written by the court.
- Resist the impulse to use a lot of quotes. Try to put the case information in your own words. This will help ensure that you understand what the court is saying.

c. Parts of a Case Brief
1. Name, date, court

2. Procedural history

3. Facts

4. Issue(s)

5. Holding

6. Reasoning

7. Disposition

8. Comments/dicta

d. Parts of a Case Brief in Detail

i. Name of the Case, Date, Court

- Use *Bluebook* or *ALWD* form where possible. Be sure to note the date of the decision. Identify the court level (trial, appellate etc.). Cross reference in the *Bluebook* or *ALWD* index to understand the hierarchy of courts if the case is from a state court.
- Understand the players.
  - Plaintiff = person who brought the lawsuit
  - Defendant = person being sued or charged criminally
  - Appellant = person who lost in lower court and brings appeal
  - Appellee = person who won below and responds to appeal
  - Petitioner = person petitioning court to hear appeal
  - Respondent = person responding to the appeal

ii. Procedural History

- Identify what occurred in the lower court to cause this case to be in the present court. Usually you can find this information at the beginning of the case.

iii. Facts

- Include facts that give the case context.
- Include the decisive facts upon which the court's holding rests. These are often found at the end of the opinion where the court gives its holding.

iv. Issue

- Identify the legal question the court is resolving. You can frame this as a question for which there is a yes or no answer.

v. Holding

- The court's decision on the question that was actually before it.
- Summarize the holding directly answers the question presented in the issue. Characterize the parties to state the decision in its broadest terms. (Example: Instead of "Mr. Jones can sue..." you would state the holding as "A father can sue...")

vi. Reasoning

- Identify the reasons given by the court for reaching its decision, including explicit and implicit reasoning.

- Identify what types of reasoning the court uses. The reasoning explains why the court ruled the way it did. Often the reasoning combines decisive facts and the legal issue.

vii. Disposition
- Identify what the court specifically did.
  - Did it reverse the lower court's ruling? Remand the case? Affirm the lower court's decision?
  - Understand the key terms: reverse, remand, reconsideration, affirm.

viii. The Rule
- Identify the rule from the case.
  - Combine the holding and the reasoning to ascertain the rule.
  - Determine the general legal principle that is applicable to the particular factual circumstance that the case stands for.
  - The rule may not be clearly stated, in which case you need to infer the rule by putting together the decisive facts, the holding, and the reasoning.

ix. Comments/Dicta
- "Comments" are notes you might write to yourself about something you do not understand in the case or that seems interesting or thought provoking.
- "Dicta" is extra language in the opinion that is not part of the holding. It may touch upon a legal issue, but if it does not directly address the issue before the court, it is dicta and not law.
- Dicta might be in the form of a policy statement the court wants to make.
- Dicta can sometimes be a good indication of what the court may do in future cases.

CASE FILE 1: On Your Own—Case Briefing and Close Case Reading

Using the format described above, write case briefs of *Rust v. Reyer*, *Reickert v. Misciagna*, and *Guercia v. Carter* (in case file 1).

2. Studying a Case

When judges decide cases and write opinions, they do not operate in a world untethered from particular facts, precedent, or social policy. They may conform to past decisions or decide to change old law. Every case is decided because a specific set of facts is before the court. And every case is decided within the social context and norms existing at the time an opinion is written. Opinions are not always explicit or clear, and you may have to figure out what a court is saying by studying the opinion carefully and reading between the lines for implicit reasoning.

Sometimes the reasoning the court uses seems convoluted. This may be more likely in a case where the court wanted to reach a certain result and had to bend the reasoning to get there. Sometimes courts decide cases and give very little justification for the ruling. If you are confused by a court's opinion, don't automatically assume that you are missing something. It might be that the reasoning or the holding is hard to discern. Law students are often surprised at how long it can take to read and comprehend even a short case.

> **PRACTICAL TIP**
>
> Most of the time you will read cases on screens. BE VERY CAREFUL that you read the *entire court's opinion* (the headnotes are not part of the opinion), all the way to the end. Do not skim or jump from page to page. By not reading the entire case, page by page, you run a potentially dangerous risk of missing a key point.

When you read cases online be careful that you don't miss parts. Be sure to read *everything* the court says. For example, a court may begin a case by running through the facts. However, the holding—and remember that the holding will likely appear toward the end of the case—may only rely on one or two of these facts. To understand the holding, you will need to be sure that you understand the **decisive facts**, not just the overall facts of the case. The court may acknowledge an important policy or societal concern at the end of an opinion or in the middle. Think of yourself as an investigator in the sense that you need to comb through and identify all the key points in a case that help you solve your client's problem.

3. Breaking Down a Case

a. Identifying Parts of a Case: Citation, Caption, Date, Summary, and Headnotes

Let's take a look at the *Reickert* case. To start, look at the caption and the summary:

This is the case citation. State appellate cases are published in two reporters, an official regional reporter, and an official state reporter. The first number is the reporter volume and the second number is the page number.

These are the names of the parties.

This is the date the case was decided.

The first paragraph is a summary of the case that includes what happened procedurally. The summary is written by editors, not by the court.

This is the ultimate holding— what the court did.

These are "Headnotes" written by the publisher, West (or another publisher depending on the state). Their purpose is to help with research. They are not written by the court and do not constitute the court's opinion. Neither the summary paragraph above nor the headnotes should ever be cited to or relied on as legal authority.

183 A.D.2D 151, 590 N.Y.S.2D 100

Supreme Court, Appellate Division,
Second Department, New York

Jeffrey REICKERT, Plaintiff;
Marilyn Reickert, Plaintiff–Appellant,
v.
Pasquale MISCIAGNA, et al., Respondents.

Nov. 2, 1992.

Mother and son filed action against homeowners to recover damages for personal injuries incurred by underage son after drinking at home in owners' absence. The Supreme Court, Nassau County, DiNoto, J., granted homeowners' motions for summary judgment. Mother appealed. The Supreme Court, Appellate Division, Santucci, J., held that: (1) mother failed to establish that homeowners had any knowledge of consumption of alcoholic beverages in their home by underage son and, thus, that homeowners could be liable for constructively furnishing alcohol under statute imposing liability for voluntary furnishing of alcohol to minors, and (2) mother's common-law claims did not survive settlement of son's action absent proof that homeowners had the opportunity to control son, or that they were reasonably aware of need for control.

Affirmed.

West Headnotes (3)

[1] Intoxicating Liquors

⚖ Owners or lessors of premises

Mother failed to establish that homeowners had any knowledge of consumption of alcoholic beverages in their home during their absence by underage son before he was injured from diving into swimming pool at home of son's friend and, thus, that homeowners could be liable for son's injuries for constructively furnishing alcohol under statute imposing liability for voluntarily furnishing alcohol to minors; alcohol consumed by son was brought by son or obtained by child of homeowners without their knowledge and son did not consume any alcohol at house with pool. McKinney's General Obligations Law § 11–100, subds. 1, 4.

b. The Issue

Typically, a court will specify the issue it will address and answer. Courts sometimes refer to this as the "Question Presented." Here the issue appears right at the beginning of the opinion:

> The question presented on this appeal is whether, as a matter of law, a parent can be held liable pursuant to *153 General Obligations Law § 11–100 where the parent does not actually furnish or assist in procuring alcoholic beverages to persons under the legal drinking age, but allegedly contributes to an atmosphere where alcoholic beverages were available by failing to supervise underage persons who were present in his or her residence, albeit without the parents' knowledge or permission.

Notice that the defendant has raised three issues for the court to address. Many judicial opinions address more than one issue. Often, only one of these issues will be relevant to your problem. You should carefully read the whole case, but you will focus your study of the case on the particular issue that concerns the problem at hand. In the Weston case, that issue is the meaning of "furnishing" under the New York Statute.

c. Star Pagination

"Star pagination" is a method used to indicate where the page breaks are in each of the published reports. The single star above tells you that the page number is the regional report (153). Double stars refer to the pages in the state volume. An example of both double and single stars appears in the excerpt below.

d. The Procedural History

The procedural history of the case is usually in the beginning of the court's opinion. It explains what happened in the case before it came before the appellate court and what issues the parties have raised for the appellate court's review. In the *Reickert* case, the procedural history is in the third paragraph of the opinion:

> In September 1987, the plaintiffs, Jeffrey Reickert and his mother Marilyn Reickert, commenced an action against the defendants Misciagna and Forkel. The action between the plaintiff Jeffrey Reickert and the defendants was subsequently settled. On or about November 14, 1989, the defendants Misciagna and Forkel moved separately pursuant to General Obligations Law § 11–100 for summary judgment dismissing the remaining cause of action asserted by Marilyn Reickert. Marilyn Reickert's other causes of action were previously dismissed and are not the subject of this appeal.
>
> By order dated March 19, 1990, the Supreme Court, Nassau County (DiNoto, J.) granted the defendants' motions for summary judgment dismissing the complaint and all cross-claims. With respect to the defendants Forkel, the court found that those defendants "did * * * not procure **102 for or furnish

to Jeffrey Reickert any of the alcoholic beverages which he admittedly consumed". With respect to the defendants Misciagna, the court found that they too "did not give, offer or furnish any alcohol to the * * * plaintiff or anyone else at [their] home on [that] day". Accordingly, the court held:

> "In the absence of any factual evidence to rebut that offered by *154 defendants and by plaintiff's son, himself, with regard to defendants' conduct in the light of General Obligations Law § 11–100, summary judgment in their favor is clearly warranted".

Notice that the court raises only one issue here. Many judicial opinions address more than one issue. Often, only one of these issues will be relevant to your problem. You should carefully read the whole case, but you will focus your study of the case on the particular issue that concerns the problem at hand.

CASE FILE 1: On Your Own—Deconstructing a Case

In the *Rust* case, identify the court, the parties, and the procedural history.

PRACTICAL TIP

In the appendix of your *Bluebook* under "United States Jurisdictions," or in the *ALWD Manual* in the back of the book, you will find the citation form for every state. These pages also indicate the court system's structure in a particular state and what each level of the court is called.

---

e. Distinguishing Background Case Facts Versus Decisive Case Facts

In the *Rust* case above, what follows is the court's rendition of the case facts. These paragraphs appear in the beginning of the court's opinion:

> The facts, viewed in a light most favorable to plaintiff, are as follows. When Reyer, then 17, learned that her parents were going to be on vacation over the weekend of October 7, 1989, she planned a party in their absence. Word of the party reached the ears of a high school fraternity—of which Tarantino was a member—known as the Marquis. Representatives of the fraternity approached Reyer and attempted to convince her to allow them to bring beer. Those attending the party would pay a one-time fee to receive a 16-ounce cup, allowing them unlimited access to the beer. Reyer agreed to have the beer at her party, in exchange for a portion of the proceeds.
>
> On the day of the party, fraternity members arrived with several kegs of beer, which Reyer allowed them to store in the garage. Fraternity members later set up the kegs, where they could be accessed from the Reyers' backyard. As the party started, the fraternity stationed three individuals at the entrance to the backyard, one to collect money, a second to stamp the hands of those

who had paid, and a third to hand out cups. Reyer attempted to arrange for her friends to have free beer, and she observed many of the estimated 150 underaged guests consuming alcohol. She did not herself drink or dispense beer at the party, collect money, stamp hands or distribute cups.

Later, responding to neighbors' complaints, the police arrived. Reyer and the police dispersed the party but the guests, including Rust and Tarantino, milled around in the street near Reyer's house. There, a melee erupted and Tarantino—impaired by the alcohol he had consumed at the party—punched plaintiff once in the face, severely injuring her. After the party the kegs were stored in the Reyers' garage, where they were later retrieved by the fraternity. Reyer never received the promised share of the fees, although she sought payment several times after the party. *358

The following excerpt is where the court identifies the critical facts on which it based its holding. This appears toward the end of the paragraph:

Here, Reyer allegedly gave permission for the alcohol at the party she was planning, provided storage for the kegs of beer both before and after the party, negotiated a share of the proceeds from cup sales for herself and at least attempted to arrange for her friends to drink the beer without charge. Her request for a portion of the proceeds from cup sales underscores her complete complicity in the fraternity's plans to furnish beer. As stated in plaintiff's affidavit, Reyer "chose to participate *360 in a scheme to furnish alcohol to underage individuals in return for a payment of money." Moreover, without Reyer's advance permission, the beer could not have been served as it ultimately was. Indeed, many of the 150 minors present may well not have come to the party in the first instance had they not known that alcohol would be available.

We conclude that if proven at trial, these facts could bring Reyer's acts within the meaning of "furnishing" as used in the statute.... Reyer's role could well be viewed as part of a deliberate plan to provide, supply or give alcohol to an underage person.

Notice that the court relies on only some of the facts to reach a conclusion about whether the defendant, Reyer, furnished alcohol. How do you know this? The court says, "We conclude that if proven at trial, these facts could bring Reyer's acts within the meaning on 'furnishing...'." *These facts*, as the court states, refer to those listed in the paragraph above. These are the specific facts the court uses to justify finding that the defendant "furnished" alcohol. The court is signaling the reader that these are the facts that decided the defendant's liability. Usually, the decisive facts are also part of, or indistinguishable from, the court's reasoning. (See the next section for a discussion about the court's reasoning.)

Why is it so important to know the decisive facts of the case? Because it will help you find the answer to your client's problem. Let's look at the facts of the Westons' case. You have been asked to analyze whether they "furnished" alcohol. The *Rust* case tells you certain facts (such as that the teenage host of the party gave permission for the party and stored the beer) regarding the extent of the host's awareness and deliberate planning of the party. These facts showed that Reyer "furnished" alcohol. In the Westons' case, there are also facts regarding the extent of their awareness of the party such as that they did not give permission and did not know of the party until afterwards. Once you have identified the critical facts of the opinion (or opinions), you can identify the critical facts of your case.

The opinion will contain background that gives context to the case. In *Rust*, for example, the background facts include that the incident occurred over a weekend and involved 150 guests. The court does not mention these fact as contributing to its holding, but it gives the reader context for the case. If the case were about a noise complaint, these facts could be decisive facts but here they only help paint a picture of what happened.

CASE FILE 1: On Your Own—Distinguish Background Versus Decisive Facts

Identify the background and the decisive facts of *Reickert* and *Guercia*.

f. Identifying the Court's Reasoning (IRAC)

Most court opinions follow a structure. For each issue (and often courts are addressing more than one issue in an opinion), the opinion begins by setting out the issue. Often, in conjunction with the issue, the court sets out a brief (one- or two-sentence) summary of the moving party's argument on the particular point.

This is typically followed by an explanation of the law that relates to the issue. Next the court applies the law, as it has explained it, to the facts of the case before it. Finally, the court concludes with the outcome of the case. Sometimes a court begins with the conclusion on the issue and then repeats the conclusion after the explanation of the law and the application to the facts. This structure is referred to as "IRAC"—Issue, Rule, Application, and Conclusion. In various forms, the IRAC structure is the time-tested method of reasoning through a legal problem.

Although many opinions follow the IRAC structure and include the elements described above, they don't always follow the structure or include all of the IRAC elements. When you are studying a case, you may have to hunt for the IRAC elements.

Let's look at the court's reasoning in *Reikert* as an example. We will focus only on the part of the opinion that addresses the issue in our case—the meaning of "furnishing" under the New York statute.

The question presented on this appeal is whether, as a matter of law, a parent can be held liable pursuant to *153 General Obligations Law § 11-100 where the parent does not actually furnish or assist in procuring alcoholic beverages to persons under the legal drinking age, but allegedly contributes to an atmosphere where alcoholic beverages were available by failing to supervise underage persons who were present in his or her residence, albeit without the parents' knowledge or permission.

Here the court sets out the issue ("I").

* * *

Under common law, the provider of intoxicating liquor was not held liable for injuries caused by the drinker, as "it was the drinking of the alcohol, not the furnishing of it, that was regarded as the proximate cause of alcohol-induced injury" (*D'Amico v. Christie*, 71 NY2d 76, 84-85). However, General Obligations Law § 11-101 (the Dram Shop Act) created a cause of action against one who unlawfully *sells* alcoholic beverages to an intoxicated person on behalf of a person who has sustained injury caused by the intoxicated person (*see, Delamater v. Kimmerle*, 104 AD2d 242, 244). As an exception to the common-law rule, General Obligations Law § 11-101 is to be narrowly construed (*see, D'Amico v. Christie, supra*, at 83; *Delamater v. Kimmerle, supra*, at 244).

Here, the court begins to provide the rule and explain it ("R").

In 1983, the Legislature enacted General Obligations Law § 11-100, which, "in contrast to the Dram Shop Act, impose[d] liability for injuries caused by intoxicated individuals who have not reached the legal drinking age upon persons '*unlawfully furnishing*' alcoholic beverages to them" (*D'Amico v. Christie, supra*, at 84). Specifically, General Obligations Law § 11-100 states in relevant part, as follows: "Any person who shall be injured in person, property, means of support or otherwise, by reason of the intoxication or impairment of ability of any person under the age of twenty-one years, whether resulting in his death or not, shall have a right of action to recover actual damages against any person *who knowingly causes such intoxication or impairment of ability by unlawfully furnishing to or unlawfully assisting in procuring alcoholic beverages for such person with knowledge or reasonable cause to believe that such person was under the age of twenty-one years*" (emphasis supplied).*

The crux of appellant's argument is that a parent can be held liable under General Obligations Law § 11-100 if he or she "constructively" furnishes or assists in procuring alcoholic beverages to underage persons by, specifically, failing to supervise such individuals at his or her residence. In the case at bar, the record reveals that the liquor consumed by the plaintiff Jeffrey Reickert took place only at the Forkel resi-

Here the court applies the rule to facts of Reickert's case ("A").

dence when the adult Forkels were not present. There is no evidence that the Forkels had any knowledge of, or that they had given any permission for, the consumption of alcoholic beverages by their son and his underage friends during their absence. Moreover, the alcohol which was consumed at the Forkel residence was mainly beer, which had been procured elsewhere and brought into the Forkel home on the day of the accident. Indeed, the injured plaintiff supplied himself with the two "eight packs" of beer which he consumed at the Forkel residence. The record also reveals that the injured plaintiff and his friends drank some "korn liquor" which had been previously obtained in Georgia by the Forkel's son without the knowledge of his parents. With respect to the Misciagnas, the injured plaintiff himself stated that he did not consume any alcoholic beverages while at the Misciagna house.

Here the court gives its conclusion ("C"). Note that it also reiterates the rule as it applies to the case. Thus, it is also the court's holding pertaining to this issue.

Under these circumstances, and in view of the legislative history, it is clear that General Obligations Law § 11-100 was not intended to impose liability for underage drinking which occurs upon an individual's premises without his or her knowledge or permission, or with alcoholic beverages over which he or she has no control.

IRAC is a very basic structure. You will use it in your own legal writing, but with some variation as dictated by the case you are working on. Although the structure is very similar to a court opinion, because a lawyer has different goals than a judge, IRAC is usually a scaffold that you may use in a variety of ways. Lawyers often use a slightly different structure with the acronym CREAC. This stands for Conclusion, Rule, Explanation of the rule, Application of the rule, and Conclusion (yes, Conclusion is in there twice— more on this when we break down how to write an analysis). There are many variations of the acronym for legal writing structure, including TRAC (Thesis, Rule, Application, Conclusion), BaRAC (Bold assertion, Rule, Application, Conclusion), or CREXAC (Conclusion, Rule, Explanation of rule, Application, Conclusion). These are only a few and your particular writing professor may have one that's preferred as a teaching tool. Whatever specific structure you are directed to use, the purpose for using the structure and the general elements are similar.

g. Understanding How a Court Reasons

While IRAC is the structure a court typically uses to explain a decision, how it reaches a decision usually is based on one or several kinds of legal reasoning. Understanding how courts reason through a legal problem should help you reason through your own analysis. Lawyers, like judges, make different kinds of arguments and use different kinds of reasoning depending on the case. Four types of reasoning are summarized below. Note that there are more, and court opinions often contain a combination of two or more kinds of reasoning.

- *Reasoning based on precedent (like stare decisis).* A court will apply a rule to a set of facts to reach a conclusion by looking at prior cases with similar facts and recognizing how the rule was applied in the prior cases. The court will reach a similar conclusion because the facts of the prior cases are similar enough to warrant this outcome. To justify the conclusion the court will need to show why the prior cases' facts are similar. A good example of this kind of reasoning is in *Diaz* (pages 34–36). Notice how the court uses explicit comparisons to the cases it has described:

  > Applying the above-mentioned principles and case law, we hold that the trial court correctly found as a matter of law that the defendants did not owe the plaintiffs a duty under the facts of this case. Unlike the cases cited by the parties, the crosswalk at the intersection in question was controlled by a "Don't Walk" signal. Nonetheless, the instant plaintiff chose to ignore it and proceed across the remainder of the intersection. Unlike *Sweet*, the plaintiff was not a youngster who relied on the directions of an adult. While we agree that *Sweet* is good law, we do not go as far as *Valdez* where it is implied that a duty would exist if the plaintiff interpreted the bus driver's gesture as something more than an indication that the driver would not move the bus until the plaintiff passed.

- *Reasoning based on interpretation.* Courts will also base a ruling on the language of a constitution, statute, or regulation. This type of reasoning can be combined with precedent reasoning because interpreting statutes often requires defining particular words or phrases. Courts will look at past cases where the same or similar language has been interpreted. They will analyze the "plain meaning" and they may also review legislative history to discern the legislature's intent in writing the law. Sometimes courts will use the dictionary when interpreting the meaning of a word in a statute.

  Reichert provides an example of interpretative reasoning:

  > In 1983, the Legislature enacted General Obligations Law § 11–100, which, "in contrast to the Dram Shop Act, impose[d] liability for injuries caused by intoxicated individuals who have not reached the legal drinking age upon persons '*unlawfully furnishing*' alcoholic beverages to them" (*D'Amico v. Christie, supra,* 71 N.Y.2d at 84, 524 N.Y.S.2d 1, 518 N.E.2d 896). Specifically, General Obligations Law § 11–100 states in relevant part, as follows:
  >
  > > "Any person who shall be injured in person, property, means of support or otherwise, by reason of the intoxication or impairment of ability of any person under the age of twenty-one years,

whether resulting in his death or not, shall have a right of action to recover actual damages against any person who *knowingly causes such intoxication or impairment of ability by unlawfully furnishing to or unlawfully assisting in procuring alcoholic beverages for such person with knowledge or reasonable cause to believe that such person was under the age of twenty-one years"* (emphasis supplied)....

The legislative memorandum in support of General Obligations Law § 11–100 (1983 N.Y.Legis.Ann., at 281–282) provides insight into the purpose of the statute. In comparing General Obligations Law § 11–101 (the "Dram Shop Act") with the proposed General Obligations Law § 11–100, Senator Smith noted, as ***155** follows:

> "To place upon those wishing to furnish alcoholic beverages without charge a duty to know or have reason to know the age of the person being served and the apparent condition of the person so served does not place an inconceivable burden.... To *voluntarily provide* alcoholic beverages to an under-age person who is already intoxicated is morally irresponsible behavior and cannot be condoned. The time has come for every individual to accept responsibility for an activity which most people partake in, consumption of alcoholic beverages—the responsibility as a consumer, and as a furnisher, as well."

- ***Rule-based reasoning.*** When a rule is indisputable and requires no interpretation, there is little reasoning to be done. For example, a law imposing a 55 miles per hour speed limit is a clear, objective standard. If your client was accused of driving at 80 miles per hour, there would be no need to argue about whether he violated the speed limit (if in fact he was going 80). Instead, you would give the rule (or law) and apply the conclusion. If, instead, your client was charged with violating a law that prohibited driving at an unreasonable speed, you would need to analyze for your reader what "unreasonable" means by doing precedential or other kinds of reasoning. For example, many states have a law that a driver may not drive a car with a blood alcohol count (BAC) of .08 or higher. This legal limit is a clear standard. If an individual charged with driving under the influence of alcohol had a BAC that was .12, there would be little analysis regarding the law on this point. You would simply state the legal standard as a fact. If instead the law was that a person is prohibited from driving in an impaired condition, you would have to analyze and explain the meaning of "impaired" by doing precedential or other types of reasoning.

- ***Reasoning based on policy.*** A court may derive its holding from legal authority, but it may also justify a holding based on social policy or standards. Review the last paragraph of the *Diaz* decision on pages 34–36 and reprinted below. The court says that the question of a signaler's duty concerns matters of "legal and social policies." The court is explicitly considering social norms in determining an answer in the case. Economic concerns are another way a court justifies a case's outcome.

> We agree that an injury is foreseeable here. But whether a legal duty exists involves **1234 ***802 more than just foreseeability of possible harm; it also involves legal and social policies. (*Swett*, 169 Ill. App.3d 78, 119 Ill.Dec. 838, 523 N.E.2d 594.) Here, the magnitude of guarding against the injury and the consequence of placing that burden on the defendant weigh heavily in favor of finding no duty. An adult pedestrian with no obvious impairments should be held responsible for deciding whether gestures and directions given by a motorist can be safely followed. We simply do not believe that the instant bus driver's act of common courtesy should be transformed into a tort thereby giving the plaintiff license to proceed across an intersection against a warning light and without taking any precautions of her own.

The *Rust* case also provides an excellent example of a court using policy to justify its holding:

> Underage drinking is a significant societal problem that has generated widespread concern (see, e.g., French, Kaput and Wildman, *Special Project: Social Host Liability for the Negligent Acts of Intoxicated Guests*, 70 Cornell L Rev 1058 [1985]; Comment, *Killer Party: Proposing Civil Liability for Social Hosts who Serve Alcohol to Minors*, 30 J Marshall L Rev 245, 257-258 [1996] [*"Killer Party"*]). All 50 States have set minimum drinking ages, a measure which has to some extent prevented minors from themselves purchasing alcohol at bars and liquor stores.... Those same laws, however, have proven far less effective in stopping minors from obtaining alcohol in a social setting, where it is provided to them by individuals who have little, if any, financial disincentive for doing so (*see, e.g., Killer Party, op. cit.,* at 260).

h. Deconstructing and Synthesizing Case Law to Form a Rule for Your Client's Case

Once a lawyer believes that he or she has completed the research and gathered the legal authority needed to address the client's problem, the next step is to pull the decisive facts and rules from the cases and to synthesize an overall rule. The "overall rule" is the rule or principle that will apply to the client's case and hopefully guide the lawyer toward a thoughtful prediction or a likely outcome.

A statute, regulation, or constitution can form the basis of a rule that will guide a lawyer in solving a client's problem. However, interpreting the meaning of the statute and how the statute specifically should apply to a client's problem requires going beyond a statute and involves reading cases that address the statute.

In the Westons' situation, the cases and the statute have already been researched so you do not need to do that part of the work. Now you need to figure out, based on the legal authority provided, if the Westons "furnished" alcohol under the New York statute.

i. Synthesizing Rules from Cases

A legal problem will not usually be solved by a simple black and white answer, but it can happen. An example of a simple black and white answer would be the one above involving a speed limit violation.

It is more likely that solving legal problems will involve complex research and analysis. The first step is to read and study the law. The next step is to put together the rules from the cases to form a guiding rule that can apply to your client's case. Rules can come from statutes (or regulations) or from cases. If there is no statute that applies, then the rule or rules will come from cases. In either situation, putting together slightly disparate principles to form one consolidated principle that applies to a client's problem is the next step.

Here is an example of synthesizing rules or principles:

> Imagine that you live in a town where the state legislature has made it a criminal violation to walk on a public sidewalk while texting on a mobile device. You have a client who was arrested after a police officer saw her tapping on her iPhone as she walked on a sidewalk. It turns out that she wasn't texting but instead was looking at directions to where she was going on a MapQuest application. Has she violated the statute? At first glance, it seems not. She was not "texting" per se. But what if texting was defined in the law as any form of digital communication? There are three cases that have been brought to an appellate court that deal with this statute.
>
> Case A upheld a conviction of a young man who was texting with a friend as he walked down the sidewalk. The court said that according to the plain meaning as defined in *Webster's Tenth New Int'l Dictionary* 2584 (2012), "texting" means to communicate digitally with another by text messaging. Because the young man was engaged in a digital communication with another person, the court held he was "texting" and therefore it was a clear violation of the statute.
>
> Case B reversed a conviction of a young woman who was playing an interactive game on her iPhone as she walked down the sidewalk. The court justified this by explaining that the law prohibited texting that amounts to interactive digital communication and because playing a game does not require communication with another, there was no violation. The underlying reason for the law is safety to citizens walking on the street.
>
> Case C upheld a conviction of a man who was using a smartphone to write an e-mail to another person while he was walking down the sidewalk. The court reasoned that e-mailing fits within the definition of digital communication because it involves communicating with another person and the statute does not make an exception for communication that is not contemporaneous. The court in Case C reiterated the safety concerns inherent

CASES	Case A	Case B	Case C	Commonalities
DECISIVE FACTS	D texting with a friend.	D playing a game on iPhone.	D e-mailing on a smartphone.	
RULE (holding)	Violation because D is engaged in digital communication with another.	No violation because D not engaged in interactive communication. Reasoning: It is more distracting to be in conversation with another, and a pedestrian who is communicating with another is less likely to look away and pay attention to what is happening on the street.	Violation because D engaged in communication with another even though it is not in live time. Reasoning: Reaffirmed reasoning from Case B.	Violation must involve communication with another person, even if not contemporaneous.

in distracted pedestrians engaged in digital communication with another individual.

How do we reconcile the statute and the three cases and apply them to our client's case?

First, look for the commonalities in the three cases. Here, the cases address pedestrians who are walking while doing something on their phones. But in the second case, the pedestrian is not communicating with another person, only playing a game.

Notice that in each case the common principle is that there is a statutory violation if the defendant's conduct on his or her phone *involves actual communication with another individual.*

Our client was not engaged in communication with another individual. She was using a resource on her phone to get directions. Therefore, you can predict that she likely did not violate the statute.

The synthesized rule could be:

> Under the state statute, it is a violation to text on a mobile device while walking on a public sidewalk. [cite to statute] "Texting" requires communication with another individual. [cite] Interacting with a smartphone in a manner that does not involve communication with another is not a violation. [cite to cases]

ii. Identifying the Court's Reasoning

When courts decide cases, often they will specifically explain why the decision is justified. The court in Case A, above, gives no reasoning for its decisions. Case B contains reasoning and Case C reaffirms it, notes the absence of exceptions, and does not add to it. Here, the justification for finding no violation in Case B is that an interactive game is less distracting (whether you agree with that or not!). The synthesized rule together with the reasoning would look like this (the reasoning is italicized):

> Under the state statute, it is a violation to text on a mobile device while walking on a public sidewalk. "Texting" to requires communication with another individual. Interacting with the smartphone in a manner that does not involve communication with another is not a violation *because it is less likely to be a distraction to a pedestrian.*

Based on this rule, our client's conduct does not seem to violate the statute.

Synthesizing the law and reconciling legal principles from a number of authorities is at the heart of what lawyers do. By studying relevant authorities carefully, a lawyer can interpret a body of law and apply it to a client's problem. How well you can predict or argue a solution to a client's problem will depend on how well you have understood and synthesized the relevant law.

An important note about synthesizing a rule: Sometimes there is not much synthesis needed. If several cases simply restate the same rule and then apply it to similar facts, you may not need to synthesize them. Instead, you will just restate the rule that is repeated in each case. Although rules can be modified by courts as each new fact scenario comes before the court, this is not always the case. The outcome of a case can also lead to little change in the rule applied.

Finally, sometimes you will need to infer the reasons for a court's decision because the reasoning is incomplete.

CASE FILE 1: On Your Own—Synthesizing the Rule

1. For the three cases in the Weston case file, make a case chart similar to the chart above.
2. Write down a rule that addresses the meaning of "furnishing" under New York law. The rule should look like this:

> "A person 'furnishes' alcohol under the New York law when _____
> _____."

i. Identifying Decisive Facts from a Client's Case

The rule that you construct from the legal authority in the Westons' case will help to distinguish the decisive facts of your client's case. Remember that in a court's opinion there are background facts and decisive facts. The same is true of your client's case. To identify the decisive facts, you have to first study the law and figure out what the rules and decisive facts were from the cases. Once you know this information, you can identify the decisive facts from your client's case. Decisive facts are legally significant facts that will affect the outcome of the case.

CASES	Case A	Case B	Case C	Commonalities	Decisive Client Facts
DECISIVE FACTS	D texting with a friend.	D playing a game on iPhone.	D e-mailing on a smartphone.		Client looking up directions on MapQuest App
RULE (holding)	Violation because D is engaged in digital communication with another.	No violation because D not engaged in interactive communication.	Violation because D engaged in communication with another even though it is not in live time.	Violation must involve communication with another person, even if not contemporaneous.	

In the cases used for the synthesis example above (Cases A, B, and C), a legally significant fact of our client's case is that she was engaged in looking at directions on her phone, not communicating with another individual. If the facts of our client's case had included that it was a sunny day, or that the client was a tourist from Europe, these facts would not affect the outcome of the case. The synthesized rule we came up with from Cases A, B, and C helps us understand that the critical fact that led to the court's decisions involved whether the defendant was in communication with another person.

The fact that our client is looking at directions and not communicating with another leads to a probable outcome. She likely wasn't violating the statute. Thus, if the client came to us for advice, such as asking whether she should plead guilty or go to trial to fight the charge, we would advise that she likely has a good argument that she wasn't violating the statute and therefore may want to fight the charge.

Let's turn to the Westons' case. From the three cases you found, you know that the court's decisions all turned on indicia of a defendant's awareness of alcohol consumption. To identify the decisive facts from the Westons' case, look for whether there are any indicia of their awareness.

CASE FILE 1: On Your Own—Identifying Decisive Client Facts

1. Make a list of the decisive facts from the Westons' case.
2. Can you predict from this list whether they are likely in violation of the statute?
3. What if the Westons had heard from another parent that a rumor was afoot that Alice was planning a party?

CHAPTER 6

The Office Memorandum: Components

The office memorandum format is fundamental to legal writing. Its mission is to educate the reader about the issue, the facts, the likely arguments on both sides, and sometimes, next steps. The format is also frequently the basis of an e-mail or a client letter. The over-arching mission is always the same: to educate the reader about the issue. You will learn how to write an office memorandum beginning with your first "client" problem described in case cile 1. Each of the successive case files will require you to write increasingly more complex office memorandums.

Once you understand the rule (or rules) that will apply to your case and you have identified the decisive facts from your own case, the next step is to put pen to paper. For Potter's case, you are asked to write the discussion section of an objective memorandum. Case files 2 and 3 require that you write an entire memorandum. This type of memorandum is typically written "in house"; that is, as an interoffice communication. You might be asked to put the information in an e-mail or hard copy. Either way, there is a basic format to follow that is universal in the legal profession. What follows is a brief introduction to the parts of a legal memorandum. In Chapter 7 you will learn how to draft the parts.

A. PARTS OF AN INTEROFFICE LEGAL MEMORANDUM

The parts of a typical interoffice memorandum include:

- Heading
- Issue or Question Presented
- Brief Answer or Summary
- Facts
- Discussion
- Conclusion

Each part of an office memorandum has a distinct function. These will be explained below and examples will be given for each part. The parts are identified below in the sample memorandum in Chapter 2.

INTEROFFICE MEMORANDUM

Heading

To: Attorney Supervisor

From: Student Lawyer

Date: September 15, 20XX

Re: *State v. Albert*: **Relevance of Albert's prior shoplifting**

Issue (also can be called Question Presented)

Issue

In Maureen Albert's trial for theft of a ham from a Hannaford Supermarket (Hannaford), is evidence of a prior incident relevant where in the prior case Albert removed a turkey from the same Hannaford without paying?

Brief Answer (also called Summary). Note there are no case cites here.

Brief Answer

Probably yes. Evidence of Albert's earlier shoplifting incident is probably relevant under New Hampshire Rule of Evidence 404(b). Admission of prior bad act evidence under Rule 404(b) requires that: (1) the evidence is relevant for a purpose other than showing the defendant's character, (2) there is clear proof that the defendant actually committed the prior act, and (3) the probative value of the evidence outweighs its prejudicial impact. As instructed, this memo addresses only the question of relevance. Albert has made her intent an issue by specifically claiming she removed the ham accidentally. The evidence of Albert's prior shoplifting is thus likely relevant to rebut her claim that she took the ham by accident.

Facts — These are the circumstances of your client's case. Notice that there is no law cited here. Only facts from your record or file.

Facts

In November 2009, three months before the current incident occurred, Maureen Albert left the Hannaford in Concord, New Hampshire, without paying for a turkey that she had placed in the bottom of her cart. Albert returned the turkey, was warned about her behavior, and was not prosecuted.

In February 2010, Albert took a cart containing a spiral ham out of the same Hannaford without paying for it. When a Hannaford employee stopped her in the parking lot, Albert said that she left the store because she realized she had forgotten her wallet in her car. She stated that she did not intend to steal the ham and had removed it from the store accidentally.

The State has charged Albert with shoplifting for the second incident. In her trial, the State wants to introduce evidence of the turkey incident to prove that she intended to steal the ham.

Discussion — The legal analysis that supports your prediction(s). The first paragraph is an introduction or roadmap of the analysis.

Discussion

Albert's prior act involving the turkey is relevant for a purpose other than character because she raised the issue of intent, and the prior act is factually similar and close in time to the charged act. Evidence is relevant for a purpose other than character if it (1) has a direct bearing on an issue actually in dispute, and (2) a clear and logical connection exists between that act and the crime charged. *McGlew*, 658 A.2d at 1194. The trial court must make specific findings on each of these elements. *Id.*

Subheadings — These are headings that divide the analysis by sub-issues.

1. Direct Bearing on Issue in Dispute

[text omitted]

2. Clear and Logical Connection

[text omitted]

1. The Heading

The purpose of a heading in a legal memorandum (or "legal memo") is self-evident: It identifies the recipient, author, and date. The reference (Re:) line should clearly identify the client file (sometimes by a number) and the specific issue being addressed. The best practice is to be as specific as possible. Interoffice memoranda become a part of a client's file and can be resources for later research or preparation for a deposition, client meeting, trial, or appeal. Office memoranda might also be used by lawyers who are researching the same issue but for a different client. Thus, being clear in the reference (Re:) line is essential. If this line only contained "Albert Trial Issue," for example, a later reader would have to search the document to find out what the specific issue was. How you label documents is actually of critical importance. This is also true for how you save memoranda in a computer file. You want to be able to easily access the memorandum not just by client name but also by subject matter. Law offices may have very specific rules for how to label files.

EXAMPLE A: Correct heading

To: Sally Lawyer
From: Lester Associate
Date: September 10, 2013
Re: Robert Reno; # 55-211167; Contract – 2010 Employment Contract-
           Enforceability of Non-Compete Clause

EXAMPLE B: Incorrect heading

To: Sally Lawyer
From: Lester Associate
Date: September 10, 2013
Re: Robert Reno file

Notice that the specificity of **Example A** will be more easily identifiable and enduring.

2. The Issue or Question Presented

In Chapter 7 you will learn specifically how to write an issue statement. The terms "issue" and "question presented" are interchangeable in a legal memorandum. Typically, this is a matter of personal stylistic preference. This part of the memorandum identifies the exact question you have been asked to analyze. The form of the question will vary depending on the type of analysis you are doing.

For example, the memo in Chapter 2 on the New Hampshire Eviction Process did not pertain to a particular client, so the issue was simply about explicating the law—specifically how to carry out eviction proceedings.

Issue
What steps are required to initiate and carry out eviction proceedings for a tenant who has not paid rent?

If the issue relates to a particular client's legal problem, then the question presented will contain decisive facts as well as the legal question:

Issue

In Maureen Albert's trial for theft of a ham from a Hannaford Supermarket (Hannaford), is evidence of a prior incident relevant where in the prior case Albert removed a turkey from the same Hannaford without paying?

Many different kinds of legal documents begin with an issue. Memoranda or briefs to courts begin with some form of an issue. Interoffice memoranda always begin with an issue in some form. There are a number of different ways to write an issue. In the section below you will find two of these, but when you are writing one in practice you may encounter supervisors who prefer that the issue be written in a certain way. These instructions should give you a sufficient base that can be easily amended to suit different styles. Notice that the issue here contains three parts:

- First, there are facts that orient the reader to the context for the question: "In Maureen Albert's trial for theft of a ham from a Hannaford Supermarket (Hannaford)....." Sometimes these context facts will take more than just a phrase followed by a comma to explain. The context facts could be a sentence, or even two sentences, depending on how complicated the case is.
- Next, is the legal issue: "is evidence of a prior incident relevant...." Admissibility is the legal question in the case.
- Finally, a statement of the key, decisive facts: "where in the prior case Albert removed a turkey from the same Hannaford without paying?" The removal of a turkey from the same store is a key, decisive fact.

The format of an issue looks like this:

[Context facts – your client's decisive facts] "is" [legal issue] "where" [key, decisive facts]

The order of these elements can vary. The words can also vary. For example, "is" can be preplaced with "does," "can," or another similar word. "Where" can be replaced with "when," "if," or another similar word.

The issue can also start with "Whether." For example:

Whether looking at directions on a smartphone on a public sidewalk constitutes "communication" with another in violation of a statute prohibiting texting while walking.

This form can also be personal to a particular client:

Whether Jane Carter's conduct of walking on a public sidewalk looking at MapQuest directions on a smartphone constituted "communication" with another in violation of the statute prohibiting texting while walking.

> **PRACTICAL TIP**
>
> Write a draft of your issue before you begin your research. Revise the issue after your research is complete. Revise it again after you finish writing the whole discussion section. You want to begin with a question that orients you to the issue at hand so that you are reminded not to go off on a tangent. As you become more of an expert in the particular legal question you are analyzing you will be better able to draft a specific and effective issue.

An issue can be quite short or it can contain two or more sentences.

EXAMPLE: A short issue

Does Lilyview Hospital have a duty to Susan Stanford <u>for negligent infliction of emotional distress</u> where Stanford went into shock after observing medical personnel attempting to revive her son after an anesthesia alarm accidentally malfunctioned?

— Legal issue
— Decisive facts

EXAMPLE: A longer issue containing several sentences

Susan Stanford went into shock while witnessing her son go into cardiac arrest as he recovered from routine hernia surgery. Hospital personnel had to revive Stanford's son after an anesthesia pump alarm accidentally failed, allowing him to receive an overdose of intravenous morphine. In a suit for negligent infliction of emotional distress, <u>does Lilyview Hospital have a duty to Stanford for injuries resulting from this incident?</u>

— Decisive facts
— Legal issue

Both of the issues above contain the two necessary components: the legal issue and the decisive facts.

Although there are many correct ways to write an issue, there are also things to avoid:

1. Do not include excess information that distracts or obscures the point.

   EXAMPLE: An issue with too much information

   Daniel Stanford, an 18 year old, underwent routine hernia surgery at Lilyview Hospital on February 2, 2012. As he was recovering, he was hooked up to a morphine pump to control pain. His mother, Susan Stanford, sat by his bed and witnessed her son's lips turn blue and his breathing stop as a loud beeping came from the pump. Stanford now experiences headaches and insomnia from the shock of the incident. Is Lilyview liable to Stanford for these injuries?

2. Do not skimp on critical information.
3. Avoid being too general in an issue. Your goal is to identify the *precise* combined factual and legal question that you are analyzing.

EXAMPLES: Issues that are too general

What constitutes "texting" under the state statute prohibiting "Texting While Walking"?

Is Lilyview Hospital liable to Susan Stanford for negligent infliction of emotional distress?

These questions do not identify either the precise legal issue or the decisive facts.

a. How to Draft a Short Issue

One way to draft an issue is to use a template:[1]

Inquiry Word	Decisive Legal Question	Connecting Words	Decisive Facts
Does [Is/Can/Did]	Lilyview Hospital have a duty to Stanford for negligent infliction of emotional distress	Where [when/if]	Stanford went into shock after observing medical personnel attempting to revive her son after an anesthesia alarm accidentally malfunctioned?

EXAMPLE:

Inquiry word — In Maureen Albert's trial for theft of a ham from a Hannaford Supermarket (Hannaford), is evidence of a prior incident relevant — Decisive legal question

Connecting word — where in the prior case Albert removed a turkey from the same

Decisive facts — Hannaford without paying?

b. How to Draft a Longer Issue

This version of an issue contains two to three sentences that give the decisive facts in a narrative fashion. These factual sentences are followed by the legal question.

To write this version of an issue you will need to know the decisive facts. Remember that these are the facts upon which your conclusion turns. If any one of these facts changed, the answer to the issue would be different. You will also need to know the precise legal question.

EXAMPLE:

Maureen Albert was arrested for shoplifting a ham from a supermarket on February 24, 2009. In November 2010, Albert was arrested after she left the same store without paying for a turkey. Is the November 2009 incident relevant in the current shoplifting case against Albert under N.H. R. Evid. 404(b)?

The first two sentences contain the decisive facts. The last sentence asks the specific legal question.

---

1. Adapted from Coughlin, *A Lawyer Writes*.

3. The Brief Answer or Summary

The brief answer or summary answers the issue and gives a quick description justifying the answer. The purpose is to tell the reader up front what the memorandum is about. A busy legal reader (and most legal readers are busy) may only look at the summary of the memorandum at first in order to get a quick idea of where the case is going. The summary should be precise, clear, and short.

PRACTICAL TIP

Once you are working in a legal office, ask to see some sample interoffice legal memoranda. These will give you an idea of the office's customs and expectations with regard to style and format. In particular, you can find out what type of issues (or questions presented) and summaries (or brief answers) the office uses.

The components of an effective summary or brief answer are:

- A quick answer. This can be "yes" or "no." Or, if your conclusion is less certain, the quick answer can reflect that. It's acceptable to say "probably yes" or "probably no."
- A summary of the rule or rules upon which your conclusion is grounded.
- A short application of the facts to the legal rule or rules.
- An alert to reader of the issues or sub-elements not being addressed in the memorandum.

The summary should not include any citations even if it refers to law from cases and statutes,[2] nor should it include background information. Being concise is never more important than in the summary.

EXAMPLE: An ineffective summary

New Hampshire's test for duty turns on whether a victim contemporaneously perceives the negligent act. To determine if a defendant is liable the plaintiff must prove that: a) the injury was foreseeable; b) the defendant was at fault; c) the accident caused the injury; and d) expert testimony exists that proves plaintiff's physical symptoms. Lilyview Hospital was liable to Susan Stanford because she witnessed her son's cardiac arrest after his hernia surgery.

> *No specific answer given*
>
> *Legal rule does not address specific issue of plaintiff's contemporaneous perception*
>
> *No clear application of client's facts*

EXAMPLE: Edited to improve effectiveness

Lilyview Hospital likely had a duty to Susan Stanford because her injuries were foreseeable and should have been prevented. The evidence is sufficient

> *Quick answer*

---

2. Because this goes against general plagiarism concerns, check with your professor to be certain this approach is acceptable.

Rule together with a
brief application of
client facts

Alert of what is not
addressed

to prove the three elements of New Hampshire's foreseeability test for duty because (1) Sanford was the mother of the initial victim; (2) she was close in proximity to the victim at the time of the accident, and (3) she contemporaneously perceived the accident when she heard the loud beep and saw her son in cardiac arrest. Since the hospital has conceded its breach caused Stanford's injury, only the duty question will be answered here.

4. The Facts

The facts section explains the background and decisive facts that lead to the legal problem. For an interoffice memorandum, the facts can be from client or witness interviews, depositions, transcripts, police reports, or documents that form the basis of the legal problem. This section contains no legal analysis. It can be organized chronologically or by topic if there is more than one issue in the case. The facts should read like a story, pulling the reader through the narrative of what happened in an easily readable format. If the facts are complex, subheadings are helpful and reader-friendly.

PRACTICAL TIP

As with the issue, it is a good idea to write a draft of the facts first and then redraft when you have completed your legal analysis. The facts section should be the last thing that you write.

It may seem odd to draft the facts section after you have a draft of the issue, summary, and discussion sections. The logic in this order is that you won't know which facts matter until you have a true grasp of the legal analysis. Once you understand the law you will know which facts are critical to your client's case—the ones that, if they were slightly different, could affect the outcome. For example, in the case involving the client accused of texting while walking, we know that what she was doing on her phone (looking at directions) is critical to the outcome of her case. The facts section of a memorandum about the texting client would need to include that detail.

Thus, the first step involves identifying the critical facts. The next step is to identify the background facts that give context to the case. For example, in the Weston case, it may not be a critical fact that the Blake's tree held special significance and value, but it helps to give the reader a picture of the event. Think about how you can paint a vivid picture of what happened. Once you have a list of background facts, make an outline that organizes the facts either chronologically or in some other logical order. Remember that you want your reader to get a good sense of the players in your case.

Any adverse facts must be included. Your analysis will address the adverse facts, most likely in your counter-analysis (see Chapter 13). Don't be afraid to acknowledge these.

Include procedural facts if the reader needs them to give context to the case. Here is an example of procedural facts from the sample memorandum in Chapter 2.

> The State has charged Albert with shoplifting for the second incident. In her trial, the State wants to introduce evidence of the turkey incident to prove that she intended to steal the ham.

Here are the steps to take in drafting the facts section:

1. Make a list of the critical facts.
2. Identify the background facts.
3. Outline the order in which you will describe the facts.
4. Draft the facts.
5. Cross-check the facts in your discussion section to ensure you have mentioned every critical fact. Do not refer to a fact in the discussion section without putting it in the facts section.
6. If your facts are long (more than three pages), consider using sub-headings.
7. Make sure that your facts tell a story. The facts should not sound like a list.
8. Revise.

PRACTICAL TIP

You may need to give citation references to the facts in a legal memo. This will depend on the type of memo you are drafting and a law office's customary practice. Sometimes office memos include a cite after every sentence in the facts. Ask to see sample memos or ask whether the facts should include citations. The *Bluebook* includes instructions for how to cite documents.

---

5. The Discussion

The discussion section of the memorandum contains the legal analysis. This is where the law that guides your answer is explained and then applied to your client's facts. If this were a math problem, this would be where you "show your work." The discussion section serves to justify the conclusion or prediction you are making about the likely outcome of the case.

Perhaps more than any other part of the legal memorandum, the discussion section usually follows a set structure. Remember the reference to CREAC in Chapter 5? The discussion section's structure and its purpose will be explained in detail in Chapter 7. For now, take a look at the discussion section of the Albert interoffice memorandum in Chapter 2. Notice that it begins with a brief introduction or roadmap. This is followed by two different sections, each with its own heading. These subsections first explain the law on the subpoint and then apply the law on the subpoint to your client's facts. They begin the section with a sentence that gives the reader a conclusion about the paragraph's point.

The discussion section is the most complex part of the memorandum and is the heart of the memorandum, which is why Chapter 7 is devoted entirely to this section of the memorandum.

6. The Conclusion

A conclusion section of a legal memo typically reiterates your overall "answer" to the client's problem. Thus, it should be a concise summary of how you think the case will turn out. Note that you do not always need to include a conclusion section. It depends on your own style and the demands of the reader for whom you are writing. Usually this section sums up the analysis and is almost a mirror of the brief answer. The two sample memos in this book show examples of both kinds of memos—one with a conclusion and one without.

A TIMELINE FOR WRITING AN INTEROFFICE MEMORANDUM
(after your research is done)

1. Draft an issue. This will likely change and be revised as you proceed in the writing process, but it's a good idea to start by writing down what the question is that you must answer. Be specific here. Remember our client who was arrested for typing on her iPhone on a street? At the outset, you could formulate an issue such as: *Does searching for directions on an iPhone while on a public street violate the "No Texting" statute?* You may revise this later, but at the outset it will help you stay focused on what you need to address.

2. Draft the discussion section. It may seem strange and out of order to write the discussion before the summary and the facts, however, the discussion section contains your legal analysis. You will need to know what is contained in your analysis before drafting the summary and the facts. Knowing the decisive facts for your case will depend on what the decisive facts were in the cases you will use. Thus, it's better to wait until you know and understand the law before drafting the facts.

3. Draft the facts. After you have a good idea about what you will say in the discussion, draft the facts section. Why? You won't know what facts will be decisive until you fully understand the legal analysis.

4. Draft the brief answer or summary. This is the last section you will write (before the conclusion). Because you have to synthesize the law and facts into a clear and concise summary, it's impossible to get this right before you have an understanding of your analysis.

5. Draft the conclusion if needed.

CHAPTER 7

Writing the Discussion Section of an Interoffice Memorandum

Writing the discussion section of a memorandum is a multi-step process, as outlined here:

1. *Identify the legal issue.* This comes after you have a good understanding of the client's facts and legal problem. Remember, as you develop your analysis, the issue will be refined.

2. *Research the law.* Once you identify the issue, look for the law that addresses the question. Often, this process will start with reading a secondary source, which will give you an overview of the relevant law.

3. *Study the law.* This is where you read and re-read cases and statutes. As you do this, you will begin to focus in on what will determine the outcome of your client's problem.

4. *Organize the information you have read.* In any given case you will probably have a number of legal authorities that together provide an answer to your client's problem. Section A, below, offers one way to organize the authorities, but it is not the only way. Ultimately, you will develop a system of organization that suits the way you think and work.

5. *Synthesize the rule.* Once you have winnowed down the authorities, you need to sketch the rule that applies to your client's case. Remember, this is what we did in Chapter 5 where we put together the statute and cases on texting on a public way.

6. *Make an outline of your legal analysis.* Every legal analysis should begin with an outline so you know how the pieces of the analysis fit together and how you will structure the analysis on the page. One suggestion for an outline format is made here, but ultimately, you will develop a style of outlining that works for you.

7. *Write a draft of the analysis.* This is where you will use some version of the CREAC structure discussed in Chapter 5.

8. *Revise the draft.*

9. *Revise the draft again as needed.*
10. *Proofread and line edit.*

We have already addressed steps 1 through 3 and step 5. You will learn about doing research in a separate course. We will now look at steps 4 and 6.

A. HOW TO ORGANIZE THE INFORMATION

One way to organize a number of authorities is to use a chart. It can help you to see the commonalities in the cases if you visually lay out the important aspects of each case. The chart below is one example of how to organize authorities. It could be expanded to include other columns, depending on the case and your personal preferences.

For example, in the Weston case, assume that you have to research each of the elements of the Social Host statute: (1) injury to plaintiff (2) by intoxicated or impaired minor; (3) intoxication or impairment of minor knowingly caused by unlawful furnishing to or assisting in procuring alcoholic beverages for minor (4) with knowledge or reasonable cause to believe the minor is under the age of 21.

Element	Rust	Reickert	Guercia	Synthesized Rule on Element
"Injury"	Decisive facts: Holding/Reasoning:	Decisive facts: Holding/Reasoning:	Decisive facts: Holding/Reasoning:	
"by minor"	Decisive facts: Holding/Reasoning:	Decisive facts: Holding/Reasoning:	Decisive facts: Holding/Reasoning:	
"knowingly caused"	Decisive facts: Holding/Reasoning:	Decisive facts: Holding/Reasoning:	Decisive facts: Holding/Reasoning:	
"reason to know minor is under 21"	Decisive facts: Holding/Reasoning:	Decisive facts: Holding/Reasoning:	Decisive facts: Holding/Reasoning:	

You will also want to develop a way to keep track of the cases. Avoid having to scroll through each case to remind yourself of what it was about. Printing out the most important cases is well worth it. Although you will continually go back to the cases, it's a good idea to have a form that you use to brief each case, or a 5″ × 7″ card for each case. The card system allows you to quickly pull out a case and see what the facts and holding were.

1. Make an Outline[1]

Often students arrive in law school unaccustomed to making an outline. In legal writing this step is critical because it forces you to think through the concepts clearly before you put pen to paper to start writing a draft. The outlining process begins during your research. You can tinker with the outline as your research progresses. Outlining will move you from analysis to writing.

When you start outlining you will probably be lost in a welter of concepts, facts, law, and reasoning. When you finish a complete outline, you will understand the analysis and have a logical, linear framework that directs you through the issues, sub-issues, rules, cases, facts, and counter-arguments to the conclusion. Then you can write efficiently.

One caveat here: For some, writing an outline is not the way to begin the process.[2] You may need to get words on a page first, what Annie Lamott refers to as the "down draft."[3] If you fit that description, try making a very skeletal outline first so you have some idea of where you are going, then go ahead and write. *But* after you finish the "down draft," you'll need to organize what you wrote. You may find that after you have downloaded your ideas on paper, you are better able to see and understand a clear structure. The danger in this method is that when you finish the down draft you may think you are done. This is very unlikely. Think of this stage as prewriting or as a "brain dump," followed by putting the text in logical order.

Outlining serves several purposes:

- Puts ideas into linear structure.
- Shows relationships between ideas; for example, which is the overarching point and which are subordinate points.
- Helps you figure out where ideas belong logically.
- Enables you to remember all the different points and nuances of an analysis.
- Can show you what you understand and where you need more thought and/or research.

---

1. The information on outlining is derived from materials by Alice Briggs, the former Writing Specialist at UNH Law.
2. See Robbins, Johansen, Chestek, *Your Client's Story*, p. 116.
3. See Lamott, Annie, *Bird by Bird*, p. 25.

2. Format

- There is no "winning" formula for the way you format an outline. It is entirely personal and should work for you.
- At a minimum, the format must distinguish between overarching points and subordinate points. Frequently ordinals (I, A, 1, a, etc.) are used to accomplish this. In other words, using bullets that simply list the points will probably not be helpful.

3. Process

- Every writer develops a personal process for outlining. There is no one right way, provided the final outline is complete and useful, and the process for getting there is efficient.
- Do not be afraid to make several outlines. This can help you learn the analysis and enables you to explore different organizations to see which works best.
- Outlining can be done in phases or iterations, as discussed below, as your understanding of the analysis develops.
- Some writers begin with all the points they want to make and organize those (bottom-up outlining); other writers begin with the major points they want to make and then add the details (top-down outlining). Many writers use a combination of these approaches.

B. A STEP-BY-STEP APPROACH TO MAKING AN OUTLINE

Step 1. Identify the major steps or ideas in the analysis.
- Frequently, this will mean identifying the rule and its elements or factors.
- For example, if the topic is "when is a prior incident admissible in a defendant's criminal trial?" the rule would have three elements: (1) the evidence must be relevant for a purpose other than showing the defendant's character; (2) there must be clear proof that the defendant committed the act; and (3) the probative value must outweigh the prejudicial impact.
- You figure out the elements of a rule by looking at how the courts approach the rule. What topics do the courts discuss? What conclusions does a court draw in reaching its holding?
- You must synthesize cases and put together a rule that incorporates new aspects to the rule that the court has added. Remember Cases A, B, and C in the Chapter 5 texting while walking case. Case C added an aspect to the rule (communication with another does not have to be live), and this should be included in the rule.

Step 2. Begin with a roadmap/global section.

- This is where you put all the information that the reader needs in order to understand the rest of the discussion/analysis.
  - If a piece of information is relevant to just one element, then it probably does not belong in the roadmap section.
  - If, however, a piece of information is relevant to the entire discussion/analysis, then it belongs in the roadmap section.
- Things to consider putting in the roadmap section include:
  - The answer to the question you've been asked.
  - The roadmap or overall rule.
  - Any interpretive standards that courts use when applying the rule. For example, do courts interpret the rule broadly or narrowly? Do courts apply the rule frequently or infrequently?
  - Any policy or purpose behind the rule.
  - Who carries the burden.
  - The relationships between elements or factors in the rule.
  - Any "givens"—that is, things that are already established or that you are not going to discuss.

Step 3. Make a section for each major step/idea/element.

- You may find as you proceed that you can combine two elements into one section, but separating them into separate sections is a good way to begin.
- Ask yourself whether each major idea/element needs to be broken down into sub-elements.
  - For example, the "relevance" element of the New Hampshire rule on admissibility of a prior incident can be broken down into two subparts (direct bearing on an issue actually in dispute, and a clear and logical connection between the prior act and the current charge). The clear and logical connection is also broken into two subparts (prior incident is factually similar and close in time).

Step 4. Put the sections into a logical sequence.

- To determine the logical sequence, first decide whether the courts typically employ a certain sequence.
- If the courts do not use a particular sequence, then ask yourself whether logic compels a certain sequence. For example, does one element depend on another? In this case the dependent element must come after the primary element.
- If neither the courts nor logic dictates a sequence, start with the strongest element or the element that is most important to the client; put the second strongest/most important element last; and put any other elements in between in descending order of importance.

Step 5. Write out the rules.
- Here is where you want to draft the rules and sub-rules.

Step 6. Indicate which case(s) you will use to illustrate/support/prove each point you need to make about the rule.
- Generally using more than one case is preferable.
- Consider using cases that show different aspects of the rule.
- Provide some citation information. These do not need to be full *Bluebook* cites; a case name and a pincite (a pincite is the specific page number where your reader can locate the cited information) or even just a case name is sufficient. Including cites keeps you from making up propositions that you can't support. It is also a useful tool when you are writing from the outline.

> **NOTE**
>
> **The next steps require going back to flesh out the outline and should be done for each section and subsection of the outline.** You may choose to complete one section before beginning another, or you may decide to put rules in all the sections before moving to the next step.

Step 7. Identify which case(s) you are going to analogize to/distinguish from your client's facts.

Step 8. Make a list of all the points that might be relevant to this discussion/argument that you have not included in the outline.
- These may be points about the law or about the facts.
- Think about each point in the context of the outline and insert it where it makes logical sense.

Step 9. Write a conclusion for each section.
- You may change this conclusion as your analysis develops.

Step 10. Check for completeness.
- At this point, stop and consider whether the rule and the cases supporting it will support all the points/arguments you want to make about your client's facts.
- If you want to make a point/argument but the rule explanation doesn't support it, then you need to expand the rule explanation.

EXAMPLE: Outline of Albert Memorandum Discussion Section: Roadmap Paragraph and Relevance

    I. Roadmap: Prior Act Evidence Admissibility
       A. Evidence is likely admissible because A:
          1. Claims accident
          2. Two acts (ham/turkey) are similar
          3. Witnesses offer clear proof A acted
          4. High probative value/low prejudicial value

     B. Rule 404(b) allows prior act evidence if:
       1. Relevant for purpose other than D's character
       2. Clear proof exists D committed acts
       3. Probative value outweighs possible prejudice to D
     C. State has burden. (*McGlew* @ 1193)
     D. 404(b) purpose is trial on merits, not character. (*Bassett* @ 893)

II. Relevance: Direct Bearing on Issue in Dispute Explained
     A. Turkey incident is relevant
     B. Evidence relevant if it has direct bearing on issue in dispute.
     C. *McGlew* @ 1194.
       1. Evidence has a direct bearing if to show absence of accident
         a. *Lesnick* admits prior act b/c D (wife) claimed stabbing of husband was accident in charged crime and prior act. (@690)
         b. *Blackey* excludes evidence because D did not claim accident. (@1334)

III. Relevance (subpart one): Direct Bearing on Issue in Dispute Applied to Albert's case
       1. Turkey has a direct bearing on whether Albert shoplifted.
         a. As *Lesnick* wife claimed two stabbings accidental; A claims both meat incidents accidental.
         b. Unlike *Blackey* D, A has claimed accident.
         c. (conclusion) Ct. will find A's claim of accident puts her intent at issue by claiming accident.

IV. Relevance (subpart two): Clear and Logical Connection Explained
       1. Clear logical connection where factually similar, close in time
         a. Precise chain of reasoning must be articulated
           i. *Lesnick* same weapon, victim, circumstances and few months apart, so prosecution could "articulate precise chain of reasoning" (@ 690)
         b. Acts must be factually similar
           i. *McGlew* no connection because different victim age, gender, and six years span between incidents, so not "clear and logical" that intent was the same (@ 1194)

V. Relevance: Clear and Logical Connection (subpart two): Applied to Albert's Case
       4. Turkey has a clear and logical connection to the charged crime
         a. Same type of product, similar removal from store, close in time; compare *Lesnick*.
         b. Unlike *McGlew* where State could not articulate precise chain of reasoning because facts too different.
         c. (conclusion) Ct. will likely find "clear and logical" connection because of similarities.

VI. Turkey Incident Meets 404(b) Relevance Requirement

CASE FILE 1: On Your Own—Outlining

Write an outline of the discussion section of the Weston memorandum.

C. EXPLAINING THE LAW IN A DISCUSSION

Good legal writing is clearly structured. When you are writing a legal analysis of an issue, first you give the explanation of the law and then the application of the law to your client's facts. The structure is not hard and fast and will vary depending on your client's problem and what you are explaining and applying.

Explaining the law to the reader requires first beginning with the overall synthesized rule. Next, you explain more specifically how the rule works. If the rule is based on a statute, then the explanation may focus on further defining terms or construction. To do this, you may have to explain cases where the court defines and applies the term to specific situations. Our analysis of whether the definition of "furnishing" applies to the Weston facts fits within this example.

If there is no statute that applies to the client's problem, the issue you are addressing may only involve explaining a rule that is based on common law cases. Or, you may be dealing with a statute where further explanation really isn't necessary.

The challenge of writing about the law is that you will need to take what can be complex concepts and explain them in simple, understandable language. Whether you are explaining the law to a client, a colleague, or a judge, you must always use plain English and strive for simple, accurate descriptions of the law.

Case file 1 gives you the chance to explain the law using a statute and three cases. You have already laid the groundwork for this by studying the statute and the cases, briefing the cases, synthesizing the rule, and outlining the analysis.

In this chapter, you will learn an approach to explaining the law. You will also learn how to apply the specific law to your client's case.

1. The Roadmap (AKA Global) Paragraph

At the beginning of a legal discussion, you will give the reader an overall roadmap of the analysis that is to come. Other terms for describing this paragraph are the "global paragraph" or the "rule(s) paragraph." Here, we will refer to it as the roadmap paragraph. If the reader had only a few minutes and wanted to quickly understand your conclusion on the issue, he or she would be able to do so just by reading your roadmap paragraph. Once the reader had more time, he or she could come back and read the remainder of the discussion.

Remember, in legal writing conclusions come first. A roadmap paragraph should begin with your overall conclusion about the case, giving your reader the prediction you are making. This is followed by the overall rule. The overall rule can come from a statute, case law, or both. The overall rule may be a synthesized rule that you have distilled from a number of cases. Next, you include policy *if* it is relevant to your prediction. Finally, the roadmap paragraph should alert the reader if there are issues that you are not going to address.

EXAMPLE: A roadmap paragraph where the overall rule comes from case law and includes policy.

Here the issue is the enforceability of a non-compete clause in a client's contract in Nebraska. A non-compete clause is a common part of an employment contract that restricts an employee from leaving employment and immediately using assets like goodwill, training, trade secrets, or client lists to compete against the employer.

DISCUSSION

The non-compete clause in Lyle Lovell's contract is likely not enforceable because it covered more geographic territory than reasonably necessary to protect Sunshine's legitimate business interest in its driver education company. Typically, a non-compete clause is only enforceable when it is (1) not greater than is reasonably necessary to protect the employer in some legitimate interest, (2) not unduly harsh and oppressive on the employee, and (3) reasonable in the sense that it is not injurious to the public. *Mertz v. Pharmacists Mut. Ins. Co.*, 625 N.W.2d 197, 204 (Neb. 2001). Failure to meet any of the three elements is grounds to invalidate the provision and reformation of unreasonable provisions is not allowed. *Vlasin v. Len Johnson & Co., Inc.*, 455 N.W.2d 772, 776 (Neb. 1990). This test promotes a reasonable balance between the employer's interests, the employee's prospects, and the public good. *See Dow v. Gotch*, 201 N.W. 655, 657 (Neb. 1924); *Am. Sec. Ser., Inc. v. Vodra*, 385 N.W.2d 73, 80 (Neb. 1986).

(margin notes: Overall conclusion; Overall rule based on common law; Policy)

EXAMPLE: A roadmap paragraph where the overall rule is based on case law and policy is not included.

This excerpt is from the sample memorandum in Chapter 2.

DISCUSSION

Albert's prior act involving the turkey is relevant for a purpose other than character because she raised the issue of intent, and the prior act is factually similar and close in time to the charged act. Evidence is relevant for a purpose other than character if it; (1) has a direct bearing on an issue actually in dispute; and (2) a clear and logical connection exists between that act and the crime charged. *McGlew*, 658 A.2d at 1194. The trial court must make specific findings on each of these elements. *Id.*

(margin notes: Overall conclusion; Overall rule from case law)

EXAMPLE: A roadmap paragraph where the overall rule is based on a statute and case law.

Here the issue is whether the client, who was having car trouble, "trespassed" when she entered a home after knocking. The homeowner had not heard the knocking and was surprised by the client inside the house.

Overall conclusion — There is insufficient evidence against our client, Ms. Carter, that she knew she was neither licensed nor privileged to enter Mr. Hall's residence, and thus a conviction against her for trespass is unlikely. Vermont's criminal trespass statute, based on the Model Penal Code, forbids an actor from enter[ing] a dwelling house, whether or not a person is actually present, knowing that [s]he is not licensed or privileged to do so. 13 V.S.A. § 3705(d) (2006). (*See also* Model Penal Code §221.2(1) (1962)). The knowledge requirement establishes a subjective standard. It is not sufficient for the state to show that the defendant should have known the entrant was not licensed or privileged to enter the dwelling. *State v. Fanger*, 164 Vt. 48, 52, 665 A.2d 36, 38 (Vt. 1995).

Statutory rule

Further statement of overall rule based on case law

CASE FILE 1: On Your Own—Roadmap Paragraph

Write the roadmap paragraph for the discussion section of the Weston memorandum.

2. Explaining the Law Using Case Examples

Once you have done an outline and constructed your roadmap paragraph, where you give the overall rule that answers the client's problem, you will, in the following paragraphs, break down the rule and show the reader how you arrived at your conclusions about the client's case. Each paragraph explaining the law should begin with a principle or focused point that you explain in the paragraph. Paragraphs in legal writing are like division problems. The answer to the particular problem is on top of the equation. The contents of the paragraph are where you "show your work" to justify for the reader that your conclusion is right.

How you "show your work" will depend on the type of problem. Typically, the explanation of the law entails using cases to show by example how the court has applied each relevant piece of the rule to different factual settings that resemble the facts of your case. Case examples are helpful in both analogizing your client's facts and distinguishing your client's facts. Remember, our system of law depends on *stare decisis*. Correctly predicting or advocating for a particular result will depend on what courts have done in the past. Thus, comparing past cases to your case is key to an accurate and thorough analysis of the law.

Each paragraph should start with the conclusion being supported or explained. Sometimes it will take more than one paragraph to explain a conclusion. In this case, use a clear transition at the start of the paragraph to alert the reader that you are continuing to support the same conclusion. Using words like "similarly," "likewise," or "on the other hand" tell the reader that you are still explaining the same conclusion as in the preceding paragraph.

3. A Step-by-Step Approach to Writing the Explanation of the Law

Step 1: Start with a principle or focused point that is a sentence or two. State the point or the legal principle that the case explanation will clarify and prove to be true. These sentences are referred to here as "focus" sentences. This sentence should be specific and should explicitly connect the reader to the part of the overall rule in the roadmap paragraph that you are addressing. You will learn more specifically how to write these sentences in Chapter 9. Use the present tense when stating the focus sentence or legal principle. Notice in the example below that the first conclusion sentence uses the same term "legitimate business interest" to alert the reader that this is the term that will be defined in the paragraph. The first sentence of the next paragraph further breaks down the meaning of "legitimate business interest" and draws the reader's attention to the definition of "unfair competition."

DISCUSSION

The non-compete clause in Lyle Lovell's contract is likely not enforceable because it covered more geographic territory than reasonably necessary to protect Sunshine's legitimate business interest in its driver education company. Typically, a non-compete clause is only enforceable when it is; (1) not greater than is reasonably necessary to protect the employer in some legitimate interest; (2) not unduly harsh and oppressive on the employee; and (3) reasonable in the sense that it is not injurious to the public. *Mertz v. Pharmacists Mut. Ins. Co.*, 625 N.W.2d 197, 204 (Neb. 2001). Failure to meet any of the three elements is grounds to invalidate the provision and reformation of unreasonable provisions is not allowed. *Vlasin v. Len Johnson & Co., Inc.*, 455 N.W.2d 772, 776 (Neb. 1990). This test promotes a reasonable balance between the employer's interests, the employee's prospects, and the public good. *See Dow v. Gotch*, 201 N.W. 655, 657 (Neb. 1924); *Am. Sec. Ser., Inc. v. Vodra*, 385 N.W.2d 73, 80 (Neb. 1986).

Overall conclusion

Overall rule based on common law

Policy

An employer has a legitimate business interest in protection against improper and unfair competition, but not against use of general skills or knowledge obtainable from a similar business. Moore, 562 N.W.2d at 540; Boisen, 383 N.W.2d at 34. *Polly v. Ray D. Hilderman & Co.*, 407 N.W.2d 751, 755 (Neb. 1987) Unfair competition is distinguished from ordinary competition by evaluating an employee's opportunity to appropriate goodwill from the employer. Boisen, 383 N.W.2d at 33. For example, in *Polly*, where an accountant had substantial personal contact with approximately 46 of his employer's accounts, the court found that the accounting firm had a legitimate interest in protecting itself against the accountant's opportunity to appropriate customer goodwill after his employment was terminated. *Polly*, 407 N.W. 2d at 756.

Conclusion sentence that focuses on one part of the overall rule—definition of legitimate business interest. Next, writer defines unfair competition. Finally, writer shows an example of how a court has applied the term "unfair competition."

Step 2: Construct your case description.
Before you write about the cases that serve as examples of how the court applies the legal principles on which you base your prediction, you need

to have done the necessary background thinking. To write an effective case description, you need to have first studied and distilled what the key cases hold. This means you must:

- Identify the court's holding (or the court's answer to the relevant legal question before it).
- Identify the court's reasoning (why the court decided the relevant legal question the way it did).
- Identify critical/legally significant facts in the case.
- Identify the legal principle that the case illustrates (the "focus sentence").

Step 3: Write the case description.

Include only critical/legally significant facts and any context facts necessary for the reader to understand the case: reasoning and holding.

Step 4: Dos and don'ts.

- DO use the past tense when describing a case.
- DON'T use party names—instead use party designations. For example, instead of using Mr. Reickert (from case file 1: Reickert case), use "plaintiff." Other designations can include "plaintiff" or descriptors such as "teen," "host," or "guest." Designating the parties by the roles they play in the case will make it easier for your reader to understand the legal principles addressed in the case.

EXAMPLE

NOT HELPFUL: Here, the writer uses names, making it difficult to discern the significance of the parties' roles.

For example, in *Polly*, where Mr. Polly had substantial personal contact with approximately 46 of Hilderman's accounts, the court found that Hilderman had a legitimate interest in protecting itself against Polly's opportunity to appropriate customer goodwill after his employment was terminated. *Polly*, 407 N.W. 2d at 756.

HELPFUL: Here, the writer uses designations. Notice that significance of the parties' actions are easier to discern.

For example, in *Polly*, where an accountant had substantial personal contact with approximately 46 of his employer's accounts, the court found that the accounting firm had a legitimate interest in protecting itself against the accountant's opportunity to appropriate customer goodwill after his employment was terminated. *Polly*, 407 N.W. 2d at 756.

- Give the reader only necessary information. Don't include procedural information unless it is critical to the issue. Don't include background facts other than to give the description necessary context.

EXAMPLE

NOT HELPFUL: The procedural information here is not decisively relevant to the key issue— the enforceability of the non-compete clause.

For example, in *Polly*, the plaintiff appealed a wage collection decision of the district court sustaining the plaintiff's motion for summary judgment and the court affirmed the district court's decision. *Polly*, 407 N.W. 2d at 753. The court found that the accounting firm had a legitimate interest in protecting itself against the accountant's opportunity to appropriate customer goodwill after his employment was terminated. *Id.* at 756. The ruling was based on the accountant having had substantial personal contact with approximately 46 of his employer's accounts. *Id.*

In *Holloran*, on March 15, 1994, police found the inebriated defendant asleep in Londonderry, New Hampshire, in the driver's seat of his pickup truck with the keys in the ignition; he was awaiting a phone call from his wife to pick her up from a Tupperware party. *Id.* at 800.

> NOT HELPFUL: Reader does not need to know the date or the exact place where the incident occurred.

- When using more than one case to illustrate the legal principle, be sure to connect the cases, making it clear to the reader why the cases are being addressed within the same paragraph (or paragraphs) to prove a principle. Using words like "similarly," "likewise," or "in contrast" alerts your reader about how the cases should be read together.
- Avoid writing a report of cases. Remember that the reader needs more than just what each case said. The reader needs to understand the principle and the cases help exemplify those principles. If each paragraph begins with "In [case name]" the reader has no context for why the case is relevant.

Evidence of a prior act is relevant to refute a defendant's claim that the crime was committed by accident. *Lesnick*, 677 A.2d at 690. For example, the court in *Lesnick* admitted evidence of a prior act because it was relevant to show the absence of an accident where the defendant claimed she had stabbed her husband in self-defense because she believed him to be an unknown intruder. *Id.* In contrast, where the defendant denied any involvement at all in the crime, the court excluded the evidence. *State v. Blackey*, 623 A.2d 1331, 1332-33 (N.H. 1993). The evidence was not relevant because, by denying the crime altogether, the defendant had not placed her intent at issue. *Id.*

> HELPFUL: Sentence that identifies the legal principle described in the paragraph below.
>
> Court's holding
>
> Court's reasoning

CASE FILE 1: On Your Own—Write a Case Example

Write a paragraph that uses *Reickert* to illustrate a legal principle.

- Start with the legal principle that the case description will clarify or prove.
- Include the relevant, legally significant facts.
- Include the court's holding on the legal principle.
- Include the court's reasoning.
- If you think more than one case supports the principle, complete the paragraph using additional cases.

D. APPLYING THE LAW IN A DISCUSSION

Because our legal system is grounded in *stare decisis,* legal analysis is typically supported by precedent cases. Ultimately whoever reads your analysis will want assurance that there is ample support for the prediction you are making. The reader will want to see that you are a reliable legal analyst. Judges have a particular reason for wanting to get the law right—they want to exercise their judgment fairly. Although your first internships and summer jobs may not require you to write a persuasive analysis for a judge, your supervisors may use the work you do to persuade a judge of a particular position on behalf of a client. Your analysis may also be needed to demonstrate to a client that a particular position is supported. Here, too, you will need ample precedent to justify your position.

Explaining the law, using specific examples of how courts have applied legal principles to problems similar to the client's, is the first step in an effective legal analysis. The next step is showing the reader *why* the prior cases support your prediction. Writing case comparisons requires explicitness and precision. Broad legal conclusions without specific support are of no use to the reader. This section will provide you with an approach to writing a precise, useful case comparison.

Effective case comparisons require that you know your client's facts. You will need to comb through the client facts and identify those that matter to an outcome. Similar to the decisive facts cited by the court in an opinion, your client's decisive facts are the ones that decide the issue. Refer to discussion about background versus decisive facts in Chapter 5. Take away a particular fact, and the outcome changes. You won't be able to judge the relevant client facts until you know the law. Once you understand the law, you can figure out which facts matter by comparing client facts to the critical facts from cases.

The application of the law to your client's problem builds upon the explanation of the relevant law. The explanation of the law and the application should form a parallel structure. The case examples you use to show how a court has applied the rule in other situations should match up with the facts you are focusing on in your client's case. Thus, once you have the explanation of the law done, you can begin to construct your comparisons—both the analogies and the distinctions. Keep in mind the legal rule that will be applied, the court's reasoning, and the outcome you are predicting as you proceed through the following steps.

1. Identify critical/legally significant facts in the prior case (i.e., the one you're using to make the analogy). Remember, these are the facts on which the court's holding turns.
2. Identify critical/legally significant facts in your client's case.
3. Identify how the critical facts make your case similar to or different from the prior case. Important note: If you can't make a direct, one-to-one fact comparison, you may still be able to make the analogy or distinction by focusing on a different level of comparison; for example, you can't compare apples to oranges, but at a higher level, both are fruit. The case facts may also be so different that they help prove your point. For example, let's say in the Weston case there was an opinion, we will call it Case A, where the defendants had gone away for the

weekend leaving their teenage children at home. The teenagers had a party and a guest was injured after falling down some stairs in an intoxicated state. The legally significant facts of case A also included that the parents had gone away twice before and each time the teenagers had a party and the police were called. The court in case A decided that the parents were liable because they should have known, based on prior events, that their children had parties when they were away. Even though the facts are different, you can contrast, or distinguish, the Weston facts. Unlike in case A, in the Weston case there had been no prior parties and thus they had no reason to believe their daughter would have one this time. Since the court in case A found the parents liable in case A, the case would support the opposite conclusion in the Weston case.

4. Identify the legal significance of the overlapping facts. In other words, use the reasoning that the court applied in the prior decision to predict what the outcome will be when the rule is applied in your client's case.

5. Construct your comparison or distinction: Start with a sentence in which you state the point the analogy is intended to make.

EXAMPLE A: Sentence that *does not state* the point of the analogy

"Albert's case is similar to the facts of *Lesnick*." This sentence does not tell the reader the substance of why the case comparison matters.

EXAMPLE B: Sentence that states the point of the analogy

"Albert's prior act is relevant here because Albert claims she took the ham by accident." This sentence tells the reader why the comparison matters.

6. Write the rest of the analogy: Compare the critical facts in your client's case and the critical facts in the prior case. Make sure to use the appropriate level of detail. Be specific and concrete; don't include any nonessential facts.

EXAMPLE A: Analogy that lacks sufficient, decisive detail

"Like the defendant in *Lesnick*, where the prior act was admitted, here Albert's prior act should be similarly admitted." Notice that the writer is comparing broad legal concepts instead of specific significant facts.

EXAMPLE B: Analogy with sufficient, decisive detail

"Like the defendant in *Lesnick*, who admitted the stabbing but claimed it was an accident, Albert made her intent an issue by claiming she took the ham unintentionally." Notice the explicit detail.

Analogies that lack sufficient depth and detail fail to provide the reader with a reliable justification for your conclusion on the problem.

Here are some ways to help the reader understand the comparison:

    a. Place the facts from the two cases close together.

    b. Explicitly make the comparison using words like "like" or "similar to" or "unlike."

    c. Use parallel structure.

    d. Compare like items.

7. Use "because"! So much of legal analysis requires you to justify why you think a particular outcome is likely. Explain why the comparison matters by applying the reasoning from the prior case to your client's facts. In this way, you inform the reader of the legal significance of the similarity/difference between your client's facts and the facts in the prior case. For example: "Therefore, *because* evidence of the prior act is offered for a purpose other than Albert's character or propensity to steal meat, it is probably admissible." In the examples that follow, the underlined portions show the reasoning that supports the prediction.

EXAMPLE: Giving the specific reasoning that supports your prediction

> Covenants that are unduly broad in scope as to time, geography, or activity are void as a matter of public policy, because they hinder competition and free trade. *See Mertz v. Pharmacists Mut. Ins. Co.,* 625 N.W.2d 197, 204 (Neb. 2001). For example, in *Mertz,* a three-year territorial covenant was unenforceable <u>because the covenant summarily precluded all solicitation within the territory rather than being reasonably limited to those customers that he had worked with directly</u>. *Id.* at 204.
>
> The courts are likely to view Reno's non-compete restriction as overly broad and unenforceable. Like the three-year non-compete clause in *Mertz,* that was invalidated because it encompassed customers with whom the employee had never had any contact, Reno's non-compete agreement similarly includes a blanket prohibition that precludes him from soliciting new customers or new markets. <u>The court is likely to invalidate such a clause, as it did in *Mertz,* because it is not narrowly tailored to cover only those customers whom Reno had previously contacted</u>.

8. Writing an effective analogy or distinction should help you discover if you have not adequately given decisive facts from a case. The case examples and the analogies and distinctions should focus on the same facts. In other words, the case comparisons in the application of the law should use the facts described in the case explanations. The two sections should include parallel analysis.

EXAMPLE: Explanation of law and application of law—parallel structure with similar use of decisive facts

> Covenants that are unduly broad in scope as to time, geography, or activity are void as a matter of public policy, because they hinder competition and free trade. *See Mertz v. Pharmacists Mut. Ins. Co.*, 625 N.W.2d 197, 204 (Neb. 2001). For example, in *Mertz*, a three-year territorial covenant was unenforceable because the covenant summarily precluded all solicitation within the territory rather than being reasonably limited to those customers that he had worked with directly. *Id.* at 204.

The highlighted portions indicate the parallel structure. Notice that each excerpt zeroes in on specific facts.

> The courts are likely to view Reno's non-compete restriction as overly broad and unenforceable. Like the three-year non-compete clause in *Mertz*, that was invalidated because it encompassed customers with whom the employee had never had any contact, Reno's non-compete agreement similarly includes a blanket prohibition that precludes him from soliciting new customers or new markets. The court is likely to invalidate such a clause, as it did in *Mertz*, because it is not narrowly tailored to cover only those customers whom Reno had previously contacted.

CASE FILE 1: On Your Own—Write a Case Comparison

Write one case comparison that either analogizes or distinguishes Weston facts to one of the cases in case file 1.

E. ORGANIZATION: INTERNAL PARAGRAPH STRUCTURE

At this point, you have a draft of part of the analysis for case file 1. You have studied the law, completed an outline, and written a case illustration and a case comparison. As you move into drafting the complete analysis, pay attention to how the structure hangs together. You want your reader to move easily through the analysis, going from paragraph to paragraph without being interrupted by a point or sentence that does not seem to flow from the roadmap you provided in the first paragraphs of the discussion section.

Legal analysis must be tightly constructed. The structure begins with the overall paragraph or roadmap. The paragraphs that follow should flesh out the legal principles identified in the roadmap paragraph. Each of these paragraphs must be constructed carefully using language that alerts your reader to the point you are supporting. At its most basic level, your writing will have an emotional impact on your reader. A reaction of ease and confidence is what you are hoping for, not frustration and confusion.

To ensure good structure, first draft the outline (see Section B above). This will serve as a guide to keep your overall structure on target. The outline should instruct you about the order in which your points must proceed. Once you begin to draft your analysis, follow these rules when writing your paragraphs:

1. Only address one point per paragraph.
2. Separate the paragraphs that explain the law and give case examples from the paragraphs that apply the law to your client's facts.
3. Begin each paragraph with a clear conclusion that tells the reader the point of the paragraph or with an obvious transition word that signals to the reader that the paragraph is substantively connected to the one preceding.
4. Keep the paragraphs short—no more than half a page, but preferably less.

1. Writing the Paragraph's First Sentence

The point of every paragraph should appear in the first sentence. This sentence should be clear and decisive. For example, when you read the following paragraph, do you know immediately the point of the paragraph? What is the writer's conclusion regarding the substance within this paragraph?

EXAMPLE A

In *Milano*, the court held the evidence allowed a reasonable inference that the bar served the intoxicated driver alcohol despite the server's claim that she refused to sell him alcohol. *Milano*, 506 A.2d at 163, 164-165. The court reasoned that the jury could have believed the driver entered the bar sober and left intoxicated where the driver got into an accident two blocks from the bar and was intoxicated at the scene of the accident. *Id.* at 165.

Now, read the following paragraph. Can you easily discern the paragraph's point?

EXAMPLE B

Even without direct evidence of a bar's sale to a patron, a jury could find that a sale occurred from circumstantial evidence. For example, in *Milano*, the jury permissibly drew an inference that the bar sold to the intoxicated driver where the driver entered the bar sober and left intoxicated and got into an accident two blocks from the bar. *Id.* at 165. In addition, the driver was intoxicated at the scene of the accident, providing further circumstantial evidence from which the jury could infer that the bar sold alcohol to the driver. *Id.* at 165.

In Example B, the writer has decisively alerted the reader to the point of the paragraph. The sentence comfortably orients the reader. By contrast, in Example A the writer begins with a case and the reader has no idea *why* that case is being discussed. The busy reader will react more favorably when the writer carefully walks him or her through the paragraph.

Here is how you might go about developing a paragraph's decisive and clear first sentence:

1. The idea emerges in draft form.

> The New Hampshire courts look at the nature of the prior act when deciding on its admission. Cite.

What does this tell the reader about how the rule works? *(identifies nature of prior act as important)*

But what is it about the nature of the prior act that is important for the reader to understand?

2. The writer refines the point of the paragraph.

> To determine the admissibility of a prior bad act, the New Hampshire courts analyze the relevance to the current charge. Cite.

What does this tell the reader about how the rule works? *(how relevant it is)*

What is missing? *(connection to the overall rule's purpose)*

3. The writer specifically identifies the purpose of the rule and the point of the paragraph with the opening sentence.

> Courts determine whether a prior bad act is admissible by examining whether the prior act evidence is relevant because it specifically refutes the defendant's current defense. Cite. For example...

What does this tell the reader about how the rule works? *(relevance linked to refutation of defendant's defense)*

4. The writer refines and sharpens the language, making the point precise and clear.

> Evidence of a prior act is relevant to refute defendant's claim that the crime was committed by accident. Cite. For example in...

2. Using Parallel Structure

Your analysis will be organized into paragraphs that explain the law followed by paragraphs that apply the law. Even though these paragraphs are doing different things, you should use the same structure in each. This will also help your reader to easily move through your analysis. In the paragraphs below, notice the parallel structure.

EXAMPLE: Explanation of law paragraph

> Evidence of a prior act is relevant to refute a defendant's claim that the crime was committed by accident. *Lesnick*, 677 A.2d at 690. For example, the court in Lesnick admitted evidence of a prior act because it was relevant to show the absence of an accident where the defendant claimed she had stabbed

The conclusion sentence: tells the reader the legal principle you are explaining.

Case information with illustrations.

The reasoning or rationale the court gives to justify its conclusion.

her husband in self-defense because she believed him to be an unknown intruder. *Id.* In contrast, where the defendant denied any involvement at all in the crime, the court excluded the evidence. *State v. Blackey*, 623 A.2d 1333, 1334 (N.H. 1993). It reasoned that the evidence was not relevant because, by denying the crime altogether, the defendant had not placed her intent or propensity at issue. *Id.* at 1334; *State v. Whittaker*, 642 A.2d 936, 938 (N.H. 1994).

EXAMPLE: Application of law paragraph

The conclusion sentence: tells the reader the legal principle you are applying to your client's facts.

Case information where illustrations are applied to client facts.

The reasoning or rationale the writer gives to justify legal conclusion.

Albert's prior act is likely relevant here because she claims she took the ham by accident. Like the defendant in *Lesnick*, who admitted the stabbing but claimed it was an accident, Albert made her intent an issue by claiming she took the ham unintentionally. Evidence of a prior similar act is relevant to disproving Albert's claim of accident because the two similar acts close in time indicate her intent to shoplift. Therefore, because the evidence of the prior act is offered for a purpose other than Albert's character or propensity to steal meat, it probably is admissible.

CHAPTER 8

Client Letters

A. CLIENT LETTERS

Client letters can cover many topics, but there are two common types: a retainment letter and a letter summarizing the probable outcome of your client's case. The example on page 20 is the second type, where the lawyer explains the probable outcome of a client's case.

1. Organization

A client letter that gives a client a prediction in his or her case follows the basic IRAC structure that you are now used to. Below is an example with labels in the margin to identify the IRAC (or CREAC) structure.

August 20, 20XX

Carl Client
3 West Street
Town, State

Re: Liz Baker's Law Degree as Marital Property

Issue or question presented. Notice that the last sentence gives a prediction (or conclusion).

As requested, this letter will give you my opinion about whether your former wife's law degree and its attendant monetary value are marital property under our state's law. Since our last meeting, I have studied the relevant law in relation to your facts. Since you and Liz jointly decided that she should attend law school, it is likely that the degree (its value) is marital property. The valuation of the degree will have to be assessed by an expert and therefore this letter will not address that issue.

Explanation of Relevant Law

Rule and explanation. Notice how the law is explained in layperson's terms. There are no references to cases.

Marital property means all property acquired by spouses during the marriage. Earned degrees generally constitute marital property where the couple jointly decided how to develop their future earning capacity to support their family by sending one party to school. Our courts view marriage as a partnership and, when a marriage ends, each of the spouses, based on the totality of the contributions made to it, has a stake in and right to a share of the marital property. This is because that property represents the capital product of the partnership.

In cases of long-term marriages where the parties jointly decided how to raise their family, manage their future earning capacity, and had shared expectations of future material benefit, the court usually awards a sum representing the fair distribution of the professional degree. The court will also consider the sacrifices made by a spouse who did not earn the professional degree. When a supporting spouse sacrifices a career or makes a significant financial contribution toward the spouse's professional education with the expectation that both parties would enjoy material benefits flowing from the degree, the court will likely view the degree as marital property.

The Likely Outcome of This Issue

Application of the law to the client's specific facts.

You will likely be awarded a sum representing a fair distribution of Liz's law degree. You and Liz have a long-term marriage and you decided together that she would get her degree first while you managed the home and the children. In addition, you sacrificed by putting off attending graduate school. Because you and Liz jointly agreed on this course of action for the benefit of the family, the court will likely award you a fair distribution of the degree. Liz's attorney will likely argue that the future monetary value is uncertain and unquantifiable. However, the court has rejected this argument in cases similar to yours. Moreover, if we have a credible expert to calculate the degree's value, the court is likely to accept our position.

Conclusion and Next Steps

Conclusion and follow-up steps.

Based on my preliminary research, it appears that Liz's law degree will be a marital asset. Our next step is to discuss hiring an expert to value the degree. These experts can be expensive, so we should discuss whether you would like to pursue this course. I suggest sending Liz's lawyer a letter outlining our position on her law degree. Perhaps we can resolve this aspect of your divorce through negotiation and agreement. Let me know if you have any questions or concern.

Sincerely,
Lawyer

2. Content

Your reader may be another lawyer, a sophisticated government official, a businessperson, or a layperson. Frequently, several people with varying backgrounds may read your letter—a board of directors or a group of small business owners or planning board members. Write so that your reader(s) can understand you. Keep in mind that client letters also serve as a helpful summary of the case. If you are working on a complex case that stretches over a long period of time, the client letters can serve as helpful tools to remember what has happened in the case.

Tailor the tone of your letter to your relationship with the client. Be respectful, specific, and candid. Keep in mind that you are a professional; do not use slang or text-messaging shorthands; be direct.

Write in plain English, avoid legalese, and keep sentences short and concise. Use short paragraphs. Your reader should be able to understand your writing without asking for an explanation. Avoid all ambiguities.

3. Retainment Letters

When a client hires a lawyer, typically the terms of the engagement are set forth in a retainment letter. The letter, very much like a contract, usually sets out what services the lawyer will perform and at what cost. Law firms and individual lawyers often have standard retention letters that are personalized for individual cases.

B. E-MAIL CORRESPONDENCE FORMAT

Lawyers communicate primarily by e-mail, whether it is with a client, another lawyer, or other professional. You will likely communicate with prospective employers via e-mail as early as the winter of your first year in law school. In law school, you will e-mail your professors, the law school staff, and fellow students. Here are a few rules of the road to follow:

1. *E-mail with your professors and the law school staff.* Treat all communication with law school personnel (faculty and staff) as professional correspondence. This is a good time to practice good e-mail habits. Here are some guidelines:
   - Identify the content of the e-mail with a proper subject line. Do not find an old e-mail with an unrelated subject and reply to it without changing the subject line. Format the subject line properly. Use capital letters and a brief (one to four words) description of the e-mail's nature.
   - Use a proper salutation, as in "Dear Professor Carter" or "Dear Ms. Jones" (if it is a staff member).

- Use proper English in the body of the e-mail. Do not use abbreviations, slang, or text-messaging shorthands, but also do not be overly formal or use legal jargon.
- Use a proper closing such as "Thank you" and a complete signature line.
- Proofread carefully. It will matter to your recipient and reflect poorly on your abilities if he or she receives an e-mail that has typos or misspellings.
- Be respectful and deferential in your tone.

2. ***E-mail with clients or other lawyers.*** You will likely begin to e-mail with other lawyers during your first year of law school. Once you are in a summer placement, you may be asked to draft an e-mail to a client or another lawyer.
   - Apply the e-mail guidelines listed above to these types of e-mails.
   - Follow the guidelines on client letters discussed in Section A above and apply them to e-mail correspondence.
   - Structure e-mails the same as letters, except that your address and contact information should be part of a signature block.
   - Include a confidentiality statement as part of the signature block. (Always check with your employer about the proper contents of your signature block.)
   - If the content of an e-mail is longer than three or four paragraphs, put the letter in PDF form and attach it to the e-mail.

A typical e-mail signature looks like this:

Susan Barkley

abarkey@workemail.com
623-233-1234 direct
623-233-2333 main
Barkley Law Offices
7 Hathaway St
Anytown, NY 23456

Confidentiality notice: This message is intended only for the person to whom addressed in the text above and may contain privileged or confidential information. If you are not that person, any use of this message is prohibited. We request that you notify us by reply to this message, and then delete all copies of this message including any contained in your reply. Thank you.

C. E-MAIL CORRESPONDENCE SUBSTANCE

Many times an e-mail to another lawyer or to a client will be for the same purpose as a legal memorandum—to offer an objective analysis of the law that predicts a likely outcome in a case. Thus, the memorandum will either be attached to an e-mail or contained in the body of the e-mail. Either way, the memorandum content that you will learn should apply or be easily adapted to the e-mail format.

D. A FINAL CAUTIONARY MESSAGE

Most employers have an e-mail and Internet policy, and you should ask to see it when you begin your employment. Employers have the right to read your work e-mails and monitor your Internet usage, and most do. More-over, your e-mails may become the subject of a request from a litigant as part of a discovery process. Thus, when you draft an e-mail, consider that your audience may end up being wider than the recipient of the message. Your reputation, credibility, and ability are all at stake with the legal cor-respondence you author. Use the *New York Times* rule on e-mailing (also known as the "Front Page of the Newspaper" test): "Don't do anything you wouldn't want published on the front page of the *New York Times.*"

CHAPTER 9

Revising

You may remember from the introduction that revising makes up a large percentage of the writing process. The different kinds of revising—large-scale, internal paragraph, and micro (grammar and mechanics)—will be discussed in this chapter.

A. LARGE-SCALE REVISING

One way to check if your analysis has a solid organization is to deconstruct it. Here is a strategy for assessing your organization.

Highlight each paragraph's first sentence, or cut and paste each first sentence into a separate document. Each sentence, standing alone, should logically show the layout of your argument. If one of the sentences lacks a clear focus, it will interrupt the logical flow of your stand-alone sentences.

Look at the sentences below. They are the first sentences from each paragraph in the sample In Chapter 2. Notice how they represent an organized logic.

Albert's prior act involving the turkey is relevant for a purpose other than character because she raised the issue of intent, and the prior act is factually similar and close in time to the charged act.

Direct Bearing on Issue in Dispute
Evidence of a prior act is relevant to refute a defendant's claim that the crime was committed by accident. *Lesnick*, 677 A.2d at 690.

Albert's prior act is likely relevant here because she claims she took the ham by accident.

Clear and Logical Connection
Next, the evidence probably meets the second prong of the relevancy analysis because a clear, logical connection exists between the charged act of stealing a ham and the prior act of taking a turkey.

Where two acts are significantly different, the court will not admit evidence of the first one to prove the defendant's intent in committing the second act.

In Albert's case, the turkey and the ham were similar products removed from the same store, using the same method of removal—all facts that show that the second incident was not an accident.

Moreover, the close time frame between Albert's two incidents further strengthens their connection.

B. INTERNAL PARAGRAPH REVISING: REVERSE OUTLINE

This strategy will help you to practice critically reading and evaluating what you have written so that you can make your document more effective. Reverse outlining gives you the real picture of your argument **as it is currently written**. By going through the task of naming what you have done and seeing the document in its true skeletal form, you can get a better perspective on what is on the page and how you can start to make it more effective. *This is a technique you can use for any writing to ensure that what you have written is what you meant to say, and to see how the parts of the writing work together.*

1. First, read the entire section (sub-issue) without stopping.
2. Re-read and note what is **actually present** in the writing (not what you think *should* be there or what you plan to have there or what was in your initial outline, unless that is exactly what is there). Describe what you see. In particular, note if you see explanation of law or application of client facts to law.
3. Note the overall point of each paragraph.
4. Note the point of each sentence in the paragraph.
5. Read the reverse outline, looking for:
   - *Organization.* Does the structure of the discussion section work logically? Is it set out in a way that the reader can follow?
   - *Content.* Do the authorities being used "flesh out" the analysis? Do the authorities used fully show the analysis?
   - *Depth of analysis.* Are cases summarized/synthesized before being described individually? Are the authorities analyzed around principles? Are decisive facts, holding, and reasoning noted where appropriate? Are facts analogized and distinguished with specificity?
   - *Gaps and ambiguities.* Having reverse-outlined the section, what gaps do you notice? Do the paragraphs include transitions and show how they relate? Does each paragraph have one main point? Do the parts of the analysis have introductory road maps? Are there inconsistencies? Are the assumptions appropriate?

C. MICRO REVISING: GRAMMAR AND MECHANICS

You may be surprised to find a section on grammar in a textbook for law students. You probably had grammar training at some point in your education, but it may have been a while ago. Consider this a refresher. Take grammar seriously. Law students juggle many new concepts as they master legal writing, which can lead to cognitive overload. The tips provided here are meant to make proofreading a bit easier, but there is no substitute for careful proofreading. A common lament of practicing lawyers is that new lawyers seem to ignore basic rules of grammar, so paying attention to the details is well worth the time.

It is important to master a few basic grammar and stylistic points. Beyond that, keep a grammar and style book handy throughout law school and into your practice.

1. Generally, avoid passive voice.
   - A "be" verb plus a past participle (a verb ending in -ed) can indicate passive voice.
     Example: Is dismissed; are docketed; was vacated = passive voice.
   - To rewrite sentences in the active voice, ask yourself, "Who is doing what to whom in this sentence?" Then rewrite the sentence to focus on the actor, the action, and the object (if there is an object).
   - The word "by" can indicate passive voice.
     Example: The sentence was commuted by the governor vs. The governor commuted the sentence.

   EXAMPLE: Sentence with passive voice

   The four factors <u>to be</u> taken into account in <u>considering</u> a request for the entry of a preliminary injunction are…

   EXAMPLE: Same sentence edited to be active voice

   A court considers four factors in deciding whether to impose a preliminary injunction. The factors are….

2. Omit surplus words
   - Replace four or five words with one or two.

   EXAMPLE: Too many words

   The fact that the court repeatedly ruled against the defendant was evidence of its bias.

   Example: Omitting the excess

   The court's repeated denials of the defendant's objections indicated its bias.

3. Use base verbs, not nominalizations
   - Legal readers want you to be clear and concrete. Use verbs to describe the action.
     Examples: act vs. action; conclude vs. making conclusions
   - A nominalization is a verb turned into a noun. You can spot a nominalization by its ending. Endings associated with nominalizations include:

-al	-ment	-ant	-ence
-ion	-ent	-ancy	-ency
-ance	-ity		

   Example: The defendant's request is that his sentence be reduced vs. The defendant requests a sentence reduction.
   - Not all words with these endings are nominalizations, and not all nominalizations are "bad." If you see a word with one of these endings, however, stop to see if you can make your sentence shorter or stronger by using a base verb instead.

4. Avoid words that lead to vague or imprecise sentences
   - There are some "buzz" words to avoid. Words like "involve," "whether," or "the court considers" inevitably lead to a sentence that does not take a position.
     Example: Decisions on preliminary injunctions involve several factors. vs. A court considers four factors in deciding whether to impose a preliminary injunction.

     EXAMPLE: Wordy

     In determining whether a suspect comprehends the consequence of the Fifth Amendment waiver, the Supreme Court does not require that every consequence <u>is known by</u> the defendant, only that the waiver <u>is made</u> voluntarily, knowingly, and intelligently.

     EXAMPLE: Better

     The Supreme Court does not require that a suspect comprehend every possible consequence of the Fifth Amendment waiver, only that the waiver is voluntary, knowing, and intelligent.

     EXAMPLE: Wordy/Imprecise

     When the defendant is a native whose language is not English, identifying a legal waiver requires looking at whether the defendant conversed freely in English during questioning, and whether the law enforcement officers understood him.

     EXAMPLE: Better

     Proof that a non-English-speaking defendant has given a knowing and intelligent waiver includes evidence that the defendant conversed freely and understandably in English during questioning.

5. Use short sentences
   - If your sentences are long, check for passive voice, nominalizations, or vague language.
   - Do a random spot-check and count words in a sentence. Average length should be less than 25 words.
   - If necessary, break up longer sentences into shorter ones.

6. Use transitions
   - Transitional phrases are used to show relationships between an individual paragraph and the preceding and succeeding ones.
   - Transitions are helpful to the reader because they provide clarity, structure, and development of the paper.
   - "Moreover," "likewise," and "on the other hand" are examples of transitional words.

7. Use Microsoft Word (or other word processing software) to fix passive voice, grammar, and style
   - Find passive voice by doing a word find for "be," "been," etc. (The search shows you where the word "be" has led to a passive construction.)
   - Be sure that your word processor options are set to identify grammar and style problems (as well as spell check).

Remember that these are tools to help you spot writing issues; however, they are not substitutes for your own proofreading and editing. This is especially true of the spell-check function. Spell-check will not always pick up a misspelled or incorrect word.

Examples of spell check errors: The court reversed defendant's motion for a new <u>trail</u>. Defendant's <u>councilor</u> was present for the police line-up.

PART III

CASE FILE 2
Mavis May

CHAPTER 10

Introduction to Case File 2

In case file 2, Lenny Hunt is suing our client, Mavis May. Hunt was injured in May's apartment while attending a study group. Mavis is a law student who also makes and sells jewelry. The night Lenny was injured, Mavis had displayed her jewelry for her fellow students to see. Hunt was injured when a tool fell on him as he leaned over to look at the jewelry.

This case file will require you to write a complete legal memo, including the issue, summary, facts, and discussion. The issue requires analysis of two sub-elements so you will have practice organizing a more complex legal discussion than you had for case file 1. Learning how to write like a lawyer is a recursive process. You will build on many of the skills you learned in completing case file 1 including:

- Close case reading
- Briefing a case
- Deconstructing and synthesizing case law to form a rule
- Identifying key client facts
- Structuring an office memo using all the parts of a memo
- Formulating and writing an issue
- Writing an outline of the discussion section
- Organizing an analysis, including explaining the rule and applying the rule
- Writing the legal discussion of an objective interoffice memo

The new skills you will learn as you complete case file 2 include:

- Compiling facts from several documents
- Understanding the hierarchy of authority in context
- Developing rules in a multi-issue case
- Writing an outline, draft, and final version of a complete interoffice memo, including a fact section and a legal discussion section
- Writing a roadmap paragraph that covers a multi-issue analysis

- Organizing two legal issues, including explaining the rule, applying the rule, and identifying how the two issues relate
- Identifying and addressing weaknesses or counter-analyses

A. THE PROCESS FOR COMPLETING CASE FILE 2 MEMORANDUM

In case file 1 there was a step-by-step process for completing the project. You will follow the same steps as you tackle case file 2. Steps 2 and 3 have been done for you, so we will begin with step 1 and then move to step 4.

1. Understand the facts of your client's case.
2. Identify the area of law that is likely to hold the answer to the legal issue in the case (e.g., employment law, medical malpractice law, criminal law).
3. Research law. This might start with reading a treatise or other secondary source.
4. Read and study relevant cases.
5. Identify the key fact from case law or the legal principles that apply to your client's problem.
6. Review your client's facts and identify the decisive facts.
7. Narrow the body of legal authority that addresses your client's problem.
8. Outline the legal analysis.
9. Begin writing process.

MEMORANDUM

To: Associates

From: Evelyn Hooper

Date: March 1, 20XX

Re: Lenny Hunt v. Mavis May—South Carolina Premises Liability Claim

I would like you to prepare an analysis of a premises liability negligence case. One of our clients, Mavis May, has asked us to represent her in defending Lenny Hunt's potential lawsuit against her. Lenny was injured in December, when he attended a study group held at May's home in Charleston. Specifically, a soldering tool fell off a shelf and hit Hunt on the head.

May, a first-year law student at Charleston Law School, lives in a large loft on the top floor of a 100-year-old, three-story building. She also has a jewelry business that she runs from her home. She has divided the loft space into separate work and living areas, but there are no doors or walls between them. There are separate private rooms, such as the bedroom, with walls and doors. Patrons and prospective clients occasionally come to May's loft to see her jewelry designs, but she primarily sells her work over the Internet and at local craft markets. May claims a federal income tax deduction for having her business in her home.

Hunt and May are members of a study group. They have been members of the group for four months. Study group members take turns hosting weekly gatherings. The host provides food and drinks for the eight to ten members who typically attend. The study group sessions usually run from 6:30 p.m. to 9:30 p.m. May hosted her first study group gathering in the second week of December. Hunt and other members of the study group strongly encouraged May to host the December meeting because they were interested in seeing her jewelry in anticipation of the holiday gift season. May states that none of the study group members explicitly mentioned buying her jewelry before they arrived at her loft.

As the study group members showed up at May's loft, May invited them to wander around her loft as she set out food and drinks for her guests. May had some of her jewelry out for display in her work area.

Hunt knew May made jewelry because she had mentioned it, and he considered buying some jewelry for his girlfriend, especially since May was willing to give discounts. Hunt wandered around the work area of the loft. In the process of leaning over to look at some pieces of jewelry, he bumped up against some wall shelves that held soldering equipment. A piece of equipment fell off a shelf and hit his head, making a deep cut above his right eyebrow. Another member of the study group took Hunt to the emergency room, where he received 21 stitches. Because of the location of the cut, Hunt required additional surgery to reduce scarring. While the scar will diminish in time, he currently has a very visible scar over his right eye.

Hunt is a 25-year-old law student of average height and build. Before his accident in December, he was in good physical shape and exercised several times a week. On the day he was cut, Hunt was casually and comfortably dressed. He was sober, drug-free, and was wearing his contacts.

Attached please find an affidavit from one of the students who was at the apartment the night of the incident.

As a courtesy, Hunt's attorney has sent us the draft of a potential complaint against May, which would be filed in the Charleston County Court of Common Pleas, a South Carolina trial court. I have attached a copy of it; it complies with South Carolina Rules of Civil Procedure. Based on a recent conversation with Hunt's attorney, and from the draft complaint, Hunt claims he was a business invitee, and that May owed him a duty of reasonable care. Apparently, Hunt claims that the study group members all talked previously about looking at and possibly buying May's jewelry when they met at her loft. May disagrees with this and stated that Hunt was not there as a business invitee, but as a social guest. May has asked us to look into this.

May would like to settle this claim, as would Hunt, and I am hoping that we can negotiate a reasonable settlement. Before I enter into negotiations though, I need you to help me fully understand Hunt's legal status when he was hurt at May's loft.

Under South Carolina law, a plaintiff must prove three elements to pursue a successful negligence claim and, specifically, a premises liability claim against the owner or occupier of land:

  (1) The defendant owed a duty of care to the plaintiff;

  (2) The defendant breached that duty by a negligent act or omission; and

  (3) The defendant's breach proximately caused the plaintiff's harm.

I would like you to focus only on the first element — the defendant's duty of care to the plaintiff.

We have represented several plaintiffs and defendants in premises liability cases, but each time the plaintiffs were customers in stores and were clearly invitees. I need to be reoriented about the distinctions between licensees and invitees in South Carolina. Please prepare an internal memorandum addressing only the question of Hunt's status and May's duty to him based on that status.

Please focus your memo's analysis on the following issues only:

  When Hunt was in May's loft, was he a licensee or an invitee?

In answering this question, please also do the following:

  Once you have determined whether Hunt is a licensee or invitee, please describe the duty of care May owed to him. For example, if you determine that Hunt was an invitee, explain what duty of care May owed to him as an invitee. Identify the facts most relevant to describing May's duty of care. Do not address whether May breached the duty.

Authorities:

Primary Authorities

We have already identified the six most helpful cases from South Carolina courts (listed in alphabetical order by the name of the first party). You are responsible for finding copies of these authorities using Westlaw or LexisNexis. You can find them in the South Eastern Reporter, Second Series, as described below. Please rely on these cases only.

Ernie Hoover v. Edna Broome, d/b/a Broome's Service Center; published in volume 479; starting on page 62; decided 10/28/96.

Nina and Charles Landry v. Hilton Head Plantation Property Owners Association, Inc. a Corporation; and Tim McBride and Ronald Malphrus, d/b/a Hilton Head Landscape Maintenance; published in volume 452; starting on page 619; decided 12/12/94.

Dorothy Neil v. Mary Frances Byrum; published in volume 343; starting on page 615; decided 4/28/86.

Perry Parker, by His Guardian Ad Litem, Nona Mae Parker v. Stevenson Oil Company; published in volume 140; starting on page 177; decided 1/28/65.

Roger Singleton, Jr. v. George D. Sherer and Julie Underwood; published in volume 659; starting on page 196; decided 2/25/08.

AFFIDAVIT

State of South Carolina
County of Charleston

My legal name is Mavis May. My current address is 5 Green Street #5, Charleston, South Carolina 29413. I am 25 years old. I am a graphic artist. I am currently also a law student. I hosted my study group in December.

I do not hold my apartment open to the public like a shopping mall or store. I do not have a sign on the street or outside my apartment announcing or advertising my business name. I only rarely sell my work directly to people who are physically present in the loft. As a member of my study group, Hunt was lawfully on the premises on December 14 and was not a trespasser. However, he was not my customer either.

Signature:

Mavis May

Mavis May

State of South Carolina
County of Charleston
Commission Exp 3.1.2022

April Hathaway

AFFIDAVIT

State of South Carolina
County of Charleston

My legal name is Dorothy Stanwood. My current address is 24 Larch Road, Charleston, S.C. I am 24 years old.

I am part of Mavis May's study group. I had heard that Mavis makes and sells jewelry. Sometime before our December meeting, I asked Mavis if I could check out her jewelry to buy. I was interested in getting holiday gifts. Mavis said that she would show us the jewelry when we came to her apartment for the study group. And, she said she'd sell to us at a discount. The night of the study group, when we arrived, Mavis told us to wander around and look at the jewelry while she prepared some snacks for us. She had the jewelry out on display.

Signature::

Dorothy Stanwood
Dorothy Stanwood

State of South Carolina
County of Charleston
Commission Exp 3.1.2022

April Hathaway

CHARLESTON COUNTY COURT OF COMMON PLEAS
CHARLESTON, SOUTH CAROLINA

LENNY HUNT,   10-CV-_____
Plaintiff,
    v.

COMPLAINT
JURY TRIAL REQUESTED

INTRODUCTION

1.   Plaintiff Lenny Hunt, through his attorneys, brings this personal injury action against Defendant Mavis May for her negligent failure to maintain reasonably safe facilities.

PARTIES

2.   Plaintiff Lenny Hunt resides at 48 North Road, Charleston, South Carolina 29401. He was injured while on Mavis May's premises, a loft, in Charleston, South Carolina on December 14, 20XX.

3.   Defendant Mavis May resides at 5 Green Street #5, Charleston, South Carolina 29413. She is a designer and graphic artist who works from her home. May sells her artwork and designs from her home.

FACTS

4.   On December 14, 20XX, May invited members of a study group to her home for a weekly meeting, starting at 6:30 p.m. May's home is also where she works.

Hunt was a member of the study group and attended the weekly gathering at May's home. Hunt arrived at May's home at approximately 6:40 p.m.

5.   Ten group members attended the gathering at May's home. May invited group members to wander around her home and look at her jewelry. She offered group members a discount for any jewelry they bought that evening.

6.   Jewelry-making equipment was placed on shelves in May's work area. Hunt was looking at May's jewelry near the shelves holding the equipment.

7.   Hunt was considering buying May's jewelry.

8.   As Hunt looked at some of the jewelry, a soldering device fell off the shelf and hit him on the head. Hunt was injured at around 7:00 p.m.

9.   As a result of being hit on the head, Hunt received a laceration above his right eyebrow. This laceration required Hunt to have 21 sutures, multiple surgeries, and extended medical treatment.

10.   Hunt suffered excruciating pain because of this injury. Hunt has also suffered facial disfigurement that will require additional medical treatment.

LEGAL CAUSE OF ACTION—NEGLIGENCE

11.   Plaintiff Hunt re-alleges and incorporates allegations in paragraphs 1-10 of this complaint.

12.   May had a duty to provide reasonably safe facilities in her loft. May owed that duty to all people legally on her premises, including Hunt.

13.   May breached her duty by permitting visitors to move around, move objects, and come in close proximity to the dangerous shelves in the work area of her premises.

14.   May breached her duty when she failed to exercise reasonable care in placing equipment on the shelves in her loft.

15.   May breached her duty when she failed to discover and remove dangerously shelved equipment from the shelves in her loft.

16.   May's breaches of her duties of care directly caused a soldering device to fall upon Hunt, resulting in extensive and continuing injuries.

17.   A person of ordinary prudence reasonably would have foreseen that a visitor such as Hunt would be injured while walking across the floor or viewing jewelry near the shelves.

18.   As a result of May's negligence in failing to provide reasonably safe facilities, Hunt has suffered actual damages. These damages include pain and suffering, disfigurement, medical bills, and related and future costs of treatment.

REQUEST FOR RELIEF

Plaintiff Hunt respectfully asks the Court to:

A.   Award Hunt more than $10,000 in actual damages resulting from Defendant May's negligence;

B.   Award Hunt pre- and post-judgment costs, interest, and attorney's fees;

C.   Grant a trial by jury; and

D.   Award such other and additional relief as this Court deems just.

Respectfully Submitted,

_____   _____
Date   Jennifer Swift, Esq.
                           Foster, Wade & Swift
                           650 Packing Street, Suite 7A
                           Charleston, SC 29401
                           jswift@FWSlawnc.com
                           843-555-8266

B. UNDERSTAND THE FACTS OF MAVIS' CASE

For case file 1, the facts were given to you in a single memo. Here, you will need to gather the facts from a few sources: the affidavits, the memo, and the complaint.

> **PRACTICAL TIP**
>
> One of the documents in case file 2 is a draft of a civil complaint. As you know from your Civil Procedure class, this is the pleading that a plaintiff files with the court to initiate a lawsuit. A complaint states the cause of action and the facts supporting the cause of action. It also contains the damages requested. A complaint is sworn to by the plaintiff, so the allegations are considered truthful. However, the complaint only represents one side's version. The opposing party files an answer (not included here) that responds to the plaintiff's allegations.

Review these documents and make notes. Until you have read the law you won't know exactly which facts are going to be critical, but you will have a good understanding of what happened to your client. Later, once you know what the rules are and how the courts have applied the rules in other circumstances, you can come back to the facts and evaluate which ones are critical to the outcome of the case (the decisive facts).

Effective lawyering requires that you keep careful notes of client and witness interviews and phone calls, as well as organized notes of what is in the client's file. A client's file can be voluminous. Most law offices have a method for keeping track of file contents. As you proceed through law school and in your summer jobs and internships, you will be exposed to these methods and will become accustomed to the practice.

At this stage, you should develop your own practice of keeping clear notes on the contents of a client's file. Case file 2 is not voluminous by any stretch, but it is a good place to start becoming an effective note taker.

1. An Approach to Note Taking

Below is one suggested step-by-step approach to note taking. As you gain more experience, you will likely personalize how you take notes.

- Read the entire file
- Organize the documents logically (either chronologically, or by subject or witness)

A suggested note-taking structure:

Who: Identify all the key players in the case and note why the person is a key player. For example, in the May case the key players are May, Hunt, and the other students.

What: The "What" contains two parts. First, note what each document is. For example, in the May case the memo that is essentially a summary of the client interview, together with the affidavits, forms the basis of your analysis. The complaint also contains useful information. For example, in the May case your notes might begin with a review of who May is, what she does, and where she lives. Go on to chronicle what happened the night of the injury. As you make these notes, identify where each piece of information comes from.

Where: This identifies the geographic location of the client's problem.

When: This is a timeline of key dates and times that are relevant to your client's case. Sometimes the dates and times that certain events took place are the most critical aspect of the case. In that situation your timeline will be more developed than where, for example, the case turns on a set of specific facts, as in the May case.

CASE FILE 2: Assignment—Review Facts from the May File

Write notes on the May file following the Who, What, Where, When format.

2. Read and Study Relevant Statute and Cases

Once you have obtained all the cases listed in case file 2 along with the statute, you will apply the methods you learned in doing case file 1:

- Read and brief each case
- Identify the relevant elements, rules, or principles

CHAPTER 11

A Closer Look at Hierarchy of Authority in Context

In Chapter 4 we reviewed the concept of Weight of Authority. Now we look more closely at how to use cases to solve a legal problem when those cases come from different court levels. Remember, your mission is to give a well-reasoned and thorough answer to the legal problem raised in the case. Finding the authority is step one (here that has been done for you). The next step is to figure out how you to use the authority to best explain your conclusion. The May case involves a South Carolina state law, so our focus will be mainly on state court decisions. However, there is one federal case in our list of cases, so we need to figure out how that fits into the hierarchy of cases.

First, let's take a closer look at how state courts are structured. Most states have several levels of courts. Generally, at the lowest level is the trial court, above that is an intermediary court, and at the top is the highest appellate court. Often there are specialized courts at the lowest level, such as family courts or probate courts. For example, below is an image of the South Carolina court system taken from the state court web site.[1] Notice that there is a supreme court, a court of appeals, and, at the lowest level, several different types of courts that have jurisdiction over specific subject matters (civil, criminal, and family, for example).

Every state's court system is different. Some states do not have a mid-level appellate court. In those states, all appeals go directly to the highest court. Some states, like New York, have confusing names for courts. New York's highest court is called the court of appeals and one of the lowest courts (at the trial level) is called supreme court.

---

1. www.judicial.state.sc.us/summarycourtbenchbook/html/generala.htm

South Carolina Judicial System

CHIEF JUSTICE
Office of Court Administration
Office of Finance Personnel
Office of Information Technology
Office of Disciplinary Counsel

SUPREME COURT
Exclusive Jurisdiction over Certain Appeals
(Death Penalty, Public Utlity Rates, Public Bonded Indebtedness, Constitutionall Challenges to Statutes and Ordinances, Elections, Orders Limiting Investigations of State Grand Juries and Abortions for Minors)
Certiorari to Review Decisions of the Court of Appeals
Certiorari to Review Post-Conviction Relief Cases
Orginal Jurisdiction

BOARDS AND COMMISSIONS
Commission on Judicial Conduct
Commission on Lawyer Conduct Office of Disciplinary Counsel
Committee on Character and Fitness
Board of Law Examiners
Board of Arbitrator and Mediator Certification
Joint Commission on Alternative Dispute Resolution
Commission on Continuing Legal Education and Specialization
Board of Magistrate and Municipal Judges Certification

COURT OF APPEALS
Jurisdiction over Appeals Not Within Exclusive Jurisdiction of the Supreme Court

FAMILY COURT
Exclusive Jurisdiction in Domestic and Juvenile Cases

CIRCUIT COURT GENERAL JURISDICTION
Common Pleas (Civil)
General Sessions (Criminal)

MASTER-IN-EQUITY
Referrals from Circuit Court

MAGISTRATE COURTS
Civil to $7,500
Criminal as Set by Statute (Generally up to 30 Days and/or $500)

MUNICIPAL COURTS
Criminal Asset by Statute (Generally up to 30 Days and/or $500)
Municipal Ordinances
Traffic Offenses

PROBATE COURT
Administration of Estates
Guardianships/Conservatorships
Mental/Substance Abuse Commitments
Minor Settlements (Under $25,000)

PRACTICAL TIP

There are two helpful and easily accessible resources for figuring out a state's court structure. First, in the back of either the *Bluebook* or *ALWD* there is a table of citations for states. You can easily identify the court levels (and proper citation) in these tables. You can also look at a state's official court Web site. These Web sites typically have a chart or explanation of the different court levels.

Typically, only appeals court opinions are officially reported. When you are researching a legal problem you will mainly study appellate court opinions; however, there may be opinions or orders from lower courts that you want to look at and use as well. State lower court opinions and orders may be available online or in hard copy at the courthouse. They will be more difficult to find, but WestlawNext does have lower court orders in some cases. You may also find relevant lower court orders by talking with other practitioners who may know about a particular case where the judge wrote an order addressing an issue you are researching. These opinions do not carry any mandatory weight with other judges, but they may have some persuasive weight, particularly if your case is before a court at a similar or lower level.

If the answer to your legal issue lies in several cases, some from a state's highest court and some from a mid-level court, how do you use these cases to explain your answer? Cases are useful to you either because they clearly set out a rule or because the court applies facts that are similar to your client's. The best cases have both: relevant facts and clear rules. If your case is in state court, here is a hierarchy to choose and rank the cases.

Best: A case from the state's highest court that is legally (i.e., the case gives the rules) and factually relevant will have the highest weight because it is mandatory authority, highly relevant, and very useful. You may use a case like this both in your roadmap paragraph and in your explanation and application of the law.

Good: A case from the state's highest court that clearly sets out a relevant rule but does not have similar facts will be useful in giving the rule, but not necessarily useful in applying your facts to the law. You could use a case like this in your roadmap paragraph, but not in your explanation and application of the law.

Good: A case from a mid-level appeals court that clearly sets out a relevant rule and where the court compares facts similar to your client's will be useful even though it is not mandatory authority. Your audience (whether it is another lawyer, a client, or a judge) will benefit from and be persuaded by knowing that another court applied facts just like your client's and came to the same conclusion you are advancing.

Good: A case from a different jurisdiction or from the federal system (if you are handling a problem in state court) that applies a similar rule to facts that are similar to your client's. Federal courts will hear cases involving state law, such as those that come before them under diversity jurisdiction[2] or federal claims that require resolution of a state law in reaching a result. These cases are not mandatory authority because they are decided under a different court system, but they can be persuasive. U.S. Supreme Court cases would be included here. Even though the case is from the highest court in the country, it is not mandatory to a state court.

---

2. Generally, diversity jurisdiction is where the parties in a lawsuit are from different states or are non-U.S. citizens.

Helpful: Trial court orders, particularly from a parallel trial court, can be persuasive though they are not binding. For example, if your case is in a state trial court and a judge from another trial court in a different county had written an order or opinion about the identical issue you are addressing, the opinion or order may help persuade the judge that your position is correct. The trick is finding the orders because often they are not reported and the only record of the opinion may be a copy in the court's file. Some electronic databases (such as WestlawNext) now include state trial court orders. Depending on the local rules of the jurisdiction you are in, you may need to append a copy to your motion or memorandum so the reader will have access to the opinion. Federal trial court orders are recorded in West's Federal Supplement Reporter (F. Supp.) and online at Google Scholar (www.scholar.google.com).

Helpful: Unpublished opinions have not been officially reported but have nevertheless been recorded, often in an electronic database such as Google Scholar, Westlaw, or Lexis, or in their own reporter (the Federal Appendix). Unpublished federal opinions can also be found on court Web sites or on PACER (Public Access to Court Electronic Records, http://www.pacer.gov). Thus, you can find them, but they are officially labeled as "unpublished." In the early 1970s, the judiciary sought to limit the number of published opinions because of the growth in appellate cases. Both to limit creation of "bad law" coming out of frivolous cases, and to reduce workloads, the courts decided that unpublished opinions would have no precedential value and thus theoretically take less time to write. However, some courts allow use of unpublished opinions. You can find out whether the court permits them by checking the court rules for the state. Federal Rule of Appellate Procedure 32.1 requires federal courts to permit nonprecedential opinions to be cited with some restrictions.

The date of an opinion is relevant to its precedential value. Newer cases that give the same rule are better than older ones because they alert the reader that the rule is recent and is still good. When a precedent is found in a very old case and in a new one, giving both cites can be useful to show that the rule has a history. There is an example of this on page 95. Notice the age of the *Dow* case that is cited with the *Vodra* case.

CASE FILE 2: Assignment—Review the Cases in the May Case

Identify the weight of each case used to support the May case.

CHAPTER 12

Developing the Rules in a Multi-Issue Case

For case file 1 you synthesized a rule for a single issue from three cases. For case file 2 you will be using the same strategies, but applying them to more cases and issues. You may want to start by making a chart for each issue similar to the chart you made for case file 1. This may seem overwhelming at first, but organizing with a chart or some other visual tool will help you tame the information, as shown below.

Status	*Parker*	*Hoover*	*Landry*	*Neil*	*Singleton*	Commonalities
	Decisive facts: Holding/ Reasoning:	Decisive facts: Holding/ Reasoning:	Decisive facts: Holding/ Reasoning:	Decisive facts: Holding/ Reasoning:		
	Decisive facts: Holding/ Reasoning:	Decisive facts: Holding/ Reasoning:	Decisive facts: Holding/ Reasoning:	Decisive facts: Holding/ Reasoning:		

Once you have identified the commonalities for each element you can develop a synthesized rule for each of the issues. These rules will be the anchor for your discussion on each issue. You completed this type of exercise for case file 1 using one element (whether or not the client "furnished" alcohol was driving). In case file 1, the legal concept you were researching was an "element" because "furnishing" is an element of the alcohol-to-minors statute. Here, the legal concepts are not elements but distinct issues. For case file 2, you will essentially write two synthesized rules and two discussions, one for each issue that you have to explain.

CASE FILE 2: Assignment—Write a Rule

Write a rule pertaining to each issue that you must explain in the May case.

A multi-element memo must start with an overall roadmap paragraph that gives the reader an introduction of what is to come in the discussion section. Then you will write a "mini-roadmap" that pertains to each element. Here is an example of an overall roadmap in a Massachusetts memo that explains the law on when custodial interrogations trigger the requirement of *Miranda* warnings:

Conclusion sentence

Introduction of the overall rule

Break down of the issues (here they are factors)

> Connor can likely show that he was subjected to a custodial interrogation by the Newbury chief of police in the absence of adequate *Miranda* warnings. Miranda warnings are necessary for "custodial interrogations." *Miranda v. Arizona*, 384 U.S. 436, 444 (1966). Custodial interrogation is questioning initiated by law enforcement officers after a person has been taken into custody or otherwise deprived of his freedom of action in any significant way. *Id.* There are four factors that determine whether an individual's freedom of action is sufficiently curtailed such that *Miranda* warnings are required: (1) the place of the interrogation; (2) whether the investigation has begun to focus on the suspect, including whether there is probable cause to arrest the suspect; (3) the nature of the interrogation, including whether the interview was aggressive or, instead, informal and influenced in its contours by the suspect; and (4) whether, at the time the incriminating statement was made, the suspect was free to end the interview by leaving the locus of the interrogation or by asking the interrogator to leave, as evidenced by whether the interview terminated with the defendant's arrest. *Commonwealth v. Bryant*, 390 Mass. 729, 737 (1984). No one factor is conclusive. *Commonwealth vs. Bryant*, 390 Mass. 729 (1984). Nor is there a specific formula to be applied. *Commonwealth vs. Haas*, 373 Mass. 545 (1977).

The remainder of the discussion section will be organized around each of the four factors. A reader-friendly way to alert your reader that you will be explaining each sub-issue individually is to divide the sections of the discussion into subsections with brief headings. Here the headings could be:

1. Place of Interrogation
2. Focus of Investigation
3. Nature of Investigation
4. Suspect's Freedom to Leave

Each of the subsections will begin with a mini-roadmap paragraph that gives the reader the rule on the sub-issue.

EXAMPLE: Place of Interrogation

Conclusion on sub-issue

> Although Connor's questioning occurred in his apartment, the court may still find that this rose to "custodial interrogation" because there were six uniformed police officers present at the time. Courts are concerned with interrogations that take place in a police-dominated atmosphere. *Commonwealth v. Shine*, 398 Mass 641, 648 (1986). *See Miranda, supra*, at 445.

Although it is less likely that the circumstances are custodial when the interrogation occurs in familiar surroundings, the courts will examine whether "a reasonable person in the defendant's circumstances would have found the setting isolating and coercive." *Breese v. Commonwealth*, 415 Mass. 249, 255 (1993); *Commonwealth v. Gallati*, 40 Mass. App. Ct. 111, 113 (1996).

Rule on sub-issue

PRACTICAL TIP

For an interoffice memo, headings of subsections should be brief. Although lawyers may have particular formats for writing headings, generally it is most helpful to the reader if the heading is one to three words. Think of headings as signposts written to alert the reader about which part of the overall rule the subsection will address.

The paragraphs that follow each mini-roadmap will further explain the rule by using case illustrations or rule-based reasoning, as appropriate, and application of the law to the client's facts.

Here is a visual of how the discussion paragraphs in a multi-issue interoffice objective memo could be organized:

Discussion

Overall roadmap: Sets out overall rule, including sub-issues. These might be elements, factors, or distinct parts of a rule.

Heading: Sub-Element 1

Mini-roadmap of sub-element 1: Sets out rule pertaining to element, factor, or distinct part.
Explanation of sub-element 1. This may take more than one paragraph depending on how many cases you need to use to illustrate the rule, or the complexity of the sub-issue.
Application of sub-element 1. As with the explanation paragraphs, this may take more than one paragraph depending on how many cases you need to use to illustrate the rule, or the complexity of the sub-issue.

Heading: Sub-Element 2

Mini-roadmap of sub-element 2: Sets out rule pertaining to element, factor, or distinct part.
Explanation of sub-element 2. This may take more than one paragraph depending on how many cases you need to use to illustrate the rule, or the complexity of the sub-issue.
Application of sub-element 2. As with the explanation paragraphs, this may take more than one paragraph depending on how many cases you need to use to illustrate the rule, or the complexity of the sub-issue.

CHAPTER 13

Counter-Analysis

The purpose of a counter-analysis is to let your reader know what the potential weaknesses are in your prediction and how you will address them. You should always have an idea about what the opposing counsel might argue, or any issues about which a court might have concerns. The counter-analysis lets your reader know that you have looked at the law from all angles and have ideas about how to approach weaknesses. Including a counter-analysis gives your reader assurance that your thinking is thorough and deep and that you have left no stone unturned.

A counter-analysis usually fits in at the end of an application-of-the-law section. Here is the counter-analysis in the sample memo in chapter 2.

> Albert's only argument in her favor likely relies on the underlying purpose of 404(b). She could argue that allowing the bad act evidence against her goes against the purpose behind 404(b) and its limitations. *Id.* at 1195 (holding purpose underlying rule 404(b) is to ensure that a defendant is tried on the merits of the case and not on character). However, the concern that a defendant not be convicted on the basis of character is met where, as here, there is a sufficient, specific purpose for its admission. By claiming that she mistakenly took the ham, Albert's placed her own intent to commit theft at issue. The prosecutor would probably be successful in arguing that the purpose of the evidence is to refute that claim and not to demonstrate her bad character.

Notice that the first sentence alerts the reader specifically that the writer is addressing weaknesses or opposing arguments. Then the potential argument is laid out followed by the legal foundation that might support it. Next the writer explains how and why the counter-argument is unlikely to succeed.

Here is another example of a counter-analysis. In this case, imagine that you are working for a prosecutor and you've been asked to write a memo predicting whether a defendant, who is charged with gun possession, can successfully move to suppress the gun on grounds that it was recovered by the police after an illegal stop and search. After researching the law, you have concluded that the police probably acted lawfully. This is the discussion section of the memo:

Overall roadmap paragraph

The police likely acted reasonably under art. 14 of the Massachusetts Constitution and the Fourth Amendment where they made a limited pat frisk of Carter after receiving information that Carter "displayed" a firearm at an after hours party and yelled to bystanders he would be back. Under art. 14 of the Massachusetts Constitution and the Fourth Amendment, police officers act reasonably when they stop and frisk a suspect after receiving information that the suspect is in possession of a firearm when the circumstances indicate a concern for public safety. *Commonwealth v. Foster*, 724 N.E.2d 357, 361 (Mass. App. Ct. 2000). An informant's report that a suspect is carrying a gun, without any other indication of danger to police or the public, is not enough to justify a stop and frisk. *Commonwealth v. Couture*, 552 N.E.2d 538, 540 (Mass. 1990). However, when the circumstances give rise to public safety concerns, the police have a duty to investigate a tip of gun possession "and may perform a pat frisk if they have a reasonable belief that the defendant is 'armed and dangerous.'" *Foster*, 724 N.E.2d at 359-60.

Explanation of the law with examples

Massachusetts courts have upheld a suspect's stop and pat frisk where the tip came from a known or anonymous source and the information involved firearms possession under circumstances indicating the suspect presented a danger to public safety. *Commonwealth v. Johnson*, 631 N.E.2d 71, 72 (Mass. App. Ct. 1994*); Commonwealth v. McCauley*, 419 N.E.2d 1072, 1073 (Mass. App. Ct. 1981). For example, in *Johnson*, the court upheld a pat frisk where a known citizen informed police a suspect was carrying a gun, and the suspect was shouting obscenities and gesticulating in an angry manner. 631 N.E.2d at 72. In *McCauley*, the court upheld a pat frisk based on an anonymous tip where the suspect was in a well-filled café at a late hour, may have been intoxicated, and had dropped his firearm repeatedly on the floor. 419 N.E.2d at 1073. The McCauley court noted that "the [late] hour, the location of the inquiry, the risks to other patrons, and the specificity of the anonymous report describing McCauley" justified the police officers' actions. *Id.*

Explanation of the law with examples

Reasonableness is at the center of any art. 14 of the Massachusetts Constitution or Fourth Amendment analysis regarding governmental intrusion of a person's body. *Id.* Where, as in *Johnson* and *McCauley*, the suspects by their conduct and manner presented a danger to others, the police had a duty to investigate a tip regarding firearm possession from a known informant or, as in *McCauley*, from an anonymous informant where the tip was specific enough to warrant reliance upon it. *Johnson*, 631 N.E.2d at 72; *McCauley*, 419 N.E.2d at 1073. Thus, the police acted reasonably in both cases when they performed a limited pat frisk of each of the defendants to uncover a weapon. *Johnson*, 631 N.E.2d at 72; *McCauley*, 419 N.E.2d at 1073.

Explanation of the law with examples

If the informant's tip merely informs police that a suspect possesses a firearm, without an indication of a threat or risk to the public, a stop and frisk is not justified. *Couture*, 552 N.E.2d at 541. In *Couture*, a store clerk called police and informed them that a customer had entered his store and "had a small handgun protruding from his right rear pocket." *Id.* at 539. Police subsequently stopped the customer based on the clerk's report of the customer's license plate, ordered him out of his truck, searched his vehicle, and discovered a .38 caliber pistol under the front seat. *Id.* In suppressing the evidence, the court reasoned the tip provided no evidence that the customer acted suspiciously in the store. *Id.* at 540. He did not threaten or intimidate the clerk; nor did he linger suspiciously or act like he was "casing the joint" in order to commit a robbery. *Id.* The only information police knew from the tip was that the customer possessed a gun in a public place. *Id.* As a result, without more, the officers' stop and seizure of the defendant, his vehicle, and his gun was unlawful where nothing indicated the customer was about to engage in illegal activity. *Id.* at 541.

Here the police likely acted reasonably when they pat frisked Carter based on the known informant's tip because the circumstances surrounding the tip likely indicated that Carter posed a threat to public safety. Like the *McCauley* case, where the police received a tip that *McCauley* had displayed a firearm late at night when he may have been intoxicated, Carter displayed a firearm in public after leaving a party in the early morning. The police in *Johnson* also acted reasonably in pat frisking the defendant after receiving a tip from a known informant that she was carrying a gun and acting belligerently. Similarly, the police here acted reasonably in pat frisking Carter because he "displayed" a firearm at an early morning hour and yelled to bystanders that he would be back. In fact, the police had a duty to investigate here, just like in the precedent cases, because the circumstances, including the defendant's conduct and the early hour, indicated a threat to public safety. Like the police officers in *Johnson* and *McCauley*, who acted reasonably under the circumstances when they made a limited pat frisk of individuals who posed a threat to the public, the police likely acted reasonably here and complied with art. 14 of the Massachusetts Constitution and the Fourth Amendment when they made a limited pat frisk of Carter based on information from a known informant that he posed a threat to public safety. *[Application of the law]*

Carter may argue that his case is like *Couture* in that there was no information other than his public possession of a firearm without any threat. This would make the stop and frisk unreasonable under the circumstances and a violation of his rights under art. 14 of the Massachusetts Constitution and the Fourth Amendment. This argument will likely fail. In *Couture*, other than the store clerk's statement that he saw the customer with a gun, there existed no additional indicia that created a concern for public safety. As the court noted in *Couture*, despite wearing the gun on his person, the defendant did not act suspiciously in the store. In *McCauley*, the court relied on "the [late] hour, the location of the inquiry, the risks to other patrons, and the specificity of the anonymous report describing McCauley" to justify the police officers' actions. Similarly, in the instant case, the hour was late, there were several people still at the party when Carter displayed his weapon and indicated he would be back, and the tip from the informant described what Carter was wearing and in which direction he had headed after leaving the party. *[Counter-analysis]*

Effective Counter-Analysis—Dos and Don'ts

- Use words or phrases to alert the reader that you are shifting to the counter-analysis. In the example above, the writer does this by saying, "Carter may argue that..."

- Be specific about the factual basis and legal grounds for a counter-analysis.

  Not helpful: Carter may argue that the police acted unreasonably in stopping and frisking him.

  Helpful: Carter may argue that his case is like *Couture*, and that there was no information other than his public possession of a firearm without any threat. This would make the stop and frisk unreasonable under the circumstances and a violation of his rights under art. 14 of the Massachusetts Constitution and the Fourth Amendment to the U.S. Constitution.

- Include the legal support for the counter-analysis. Notice in the example above that the writer shows how the *Couture* case could be used for supporting a different legal conclusion.

- Specifically refute the counter-analysis. Show the reader how you would deal with the opposing position. In the example above, the reader is clear about this when she says, "This argument will likely fail." She follows this with the specific reasons why it will fail.

Lawyering often requires advocating for a particular position. Usually there will be an opposing position. An effective lawyer can anticipate opposing arguments. You will need to feel comfortable stepping into the shoes of opposing counsel to see the legal issue from a different perspective, even as you advocate zealously for your client.

Let's return to our client in Chapter 6, the one who was arrested for texting while she walked down a sidewalk. Recall that she was looking up directions on her iPhone and not actually texting with another individual. Based on an analysis of the three cases, it looked like she did not violate the statute because she was not communicating with another person. However, what if you were the prosecutor in the case? Would you have a different interpretation? How would you argue that the defendant had violated the statute? If you were asked to draft a memo for your supervisor that analyzed whether the defendant violated the statute, you would include a section that addressed the likely arguments that the prosecutor might make. You would also address how you would refute those arguments.

CASE FILE 2: Assignment—Practice Writing a Counter-Analysis

Write a brief (one-paragraph) counter-analysis explaining what the prosecutor would likely argue in the texting case in Chapter 5. Include why that argument would not prevail.

PART IV

CASE FILE 3
Starr v. RISE UP, Inc.

CHAPTER 14

Introduction to Case File 3

Case file 3 involves an employment law issue, the potentially wrongful termination of a physician.

The case will give you an opportunity to practice the skills you have learned so far:

- Close case reading
- Briefing a case
- Deconstructing and synthesizing case law to form a rule
- Identifying key client facts
- Structuring an office memo using all parts of a memo
- Formulating and writing an issue
- Writing an outline of the discussion section
- Organizing an analysis, including explaining the rule and applying the rule
- Writing the legal discussion of an objective interoffice memo
- Compiling facts from several documents
- Understanding the hierarchy of authority in context
- Developing rules in a multi-issue case
- Writing an outline, draft, and final draft of a complete interoffice memo, including a fact section and legal discussion section

The new skills you will learn as you complete case file 3 include:

- Conducting independent research
- Applying a normative or policy analysis
- Drafting an e-mail to a client

INTER-OFFICE MEMORANDUM

To: Associate
From: Ann Freed, Esq.
Date: November 6, 20XX
Re: Starr v. RISE UP Medical Clinic

We represent Dr. Harold Starr, a local physician. He was recently arrested for DWI. He is requesting our help with a potential wrongful discharge claim that may arise in part because of the DWI arrest and other circumstances.

Dr. Starr is the Medical Director at a privately owned, for-profit, outpatient medical clinic for adolescents in Manchester, New Hampshire. The clinic is owned by RISE UP, a national chain. (See attached promotional brochure.) Dr. Starr reports directly to the Manchester clinic CEO, Steve Lowell, who fired him on August 10, 20XX. Mr. Lowell did not state a reason that day, but did so in an August 25, 20XX, letter that Dr. Starr did not receive until August 26, 20XX.

I met with Dr. Starr for approximately one hour and asked him to prepare a detailed summary of the events surrounding his discharge. After Dr. Starr sent me his summary, he forwarded the attached letter from RISE UP's corporate counsel, Atty. Wrath. It is dated September 15, more than a month after the original August 10 discharge. I have attached Dr. Starr's summary, the brochure, Mr. Lowell's letter, and Mr. Wrath's letter.

Please review these materials and do the following:

Make a decision, based on your analysis of the law and facts, about whether Dr. Starr should file a wrongful discharge claim. Write a memo explaining the law and then applying it in a manner that supports your position and also addresses the likely counter-arguments. Please write it in a straightforward manner so that I can understand your complete legal and factual analysis, but also so that Dr. Starr can read and understand it. I would like to send your memo to him.

Please keep in mind two significant factors. First, Atty. Wrath does not provide any objective documentation to support his explanation concerning the "pro bono pool." We probably will not get to see any such documents unless we file suit and engage in discovery. If a basis exists for filing suit, I will request that Atty. Wrath provide some documentation prior to our filing suit.

Second, as you can see from Dr. Starr's letter and summary, this event has severely impacted him both professionally and personally. He is relying on us to guide him wisely, so please give him a fair and balanced assessment of the law and facts so that he can make an informed decision. Thank you for your help.

RISE UP MEDICAL CLINICS
2000 RISING SUN WAY
MANCHESTER, NH 03105

REGISTERED MAIL—RETURN RECEIPT REQUESTED

Harold Starr, M.D.
123 Fourth St.
Manchester, NH 03105

August 25, 20XX

Dear Dr. Starr,

RISE UP Medical Clinics terminated your employment for cause as of August 10, 2016. The reasons for the termination are listed below.

1. Lack of personal integrity. On August 8, 20XX, you were arrested for DWI. The corporate value of integrity requires that "each employee remain substance and addiction free at all times." The clinic cannot afford to have its medical director reported in the regional paper as a criminal with a drinking problem.

2. Breach of company policy. Our corporate policy is that only the CEO has access to confidential financial information. You secretly hacked into my computer system and reviewed, printed, and distributed confidential patient financial information. This policy breach has irreparably destroyed the working relationship.

3. Insubordination. You were disloyal to your supervisor, the CEO, by failing to discuss your concerns directly with me. The RISE UP corporate value of respect demands this. You completely disregarded the longstanding working relationship we had. I am extremely disappointed in your lack of professional and personal judgment.

4. Lack of professional boundaries and ethics. You jumped to an incorrect "conspiracy" theory totally without justification. Certain clients signed a contract in which they agreed to pay a higher billing rate. Despite actually seeing these signed contracts in the file, you concocted a bizarre accusation against me. Your judgment obviously is impaired by your alcoholism, rendering your working relationship with RISE UP impossible to continue.

Regrettably,

Steve Lowell

Steve Lowell, CEO

RISE UP MEDICAL CLINICS
2000 RISING SUN WAY
MANCHESTER, NH 03105

REGISTERED MAIL—RETURN RECEIPT REQUESTED

Harold Starr, M.D.
123 Fourth St.
Manchester, NH 03105

September 15, 20XX

Dear Dr. Starr,

I have been asked to clarify the basis for the corporate decision to terminate your employment. I have reviewed your August 8, 20XX, report to the HR representative and the documents you provided to her. I have also spoken at length with Mr. Lowell and have reviewed his August 26 letter to you. Based on this investigation, I have decided that the initial termination decision should stand. The following reasons support this decision.

You are well aware that RISE UP's corporate policy is that only the CEO has access to customers' personal financial information and that all billing is handled from Indiana. You are also aware that RISE UP provides 50% pro bono care at every clinic. What you may not have known, because we are discrete about this, is that some customers express their appreciation for the help we provide their children by contributing to our corporate pro bono pool. They can do this either by making a general contribution to the national pool or by electing to sponsor care for a teenager in their own community. To effectuate an ongoing gift, some customers prefer to execute a fee agreement that simply increases their billing rate beyond the advertised minimum. All of the gift paperwork is maintained at headquarters in Indiana except that the CEO retains a copy of the individual fee agreement and the identity of the pro bono patient so that if that patient no longer needs our services, the CEO can match the gift to a different local pro bono patient. Of the 400 patients served in Manchester, 200 are pro bono patients, and we have 86 generous "matching" benefactors who prefer to remain anonymous.

The reason all billing is handled from headquarters is to assure all concerned that you and others who provide direct care will do so without regard to whether a particular patient is pro bono or from a benefactor family. In short, what you discovered when you hacked into your CEO's computer was not a scam involving corporate fraud at all, but rather a planned-giving program that operates discretely, as promised, for legitimate policy reasons.

You were an "at-will employee," which means you could be terminated at any time for any reason or no reason. Here, we have several legitimate business reasons to discharge you. First, you exercised such extremely poor judgment at each turn that it would be impossible for you and Mr. Lowell to maintain a satisfactory working relationship going forward. Effective management of the Manchester clinic requires that the CEO and Medical Director work closely together with mutual trust and respect. Given the personal and professional breaches here, that is no longer possible.

Second, you violated corporate policy by examining numerous customers' confidential documents. If your purpose really was to correct an isolated billing problem for Mr. Howard, all you needed to do was ask Mr. Lowell a simple question face-to-face on his return. However, despite your 29-year working relationship with Mr. Lowell, you did not trust or respect him enough to address your concerns with him directly.

Even putting aside your enormous lapse in judgment in getting arrested for DWI as a Medical Director who counsels substance-abuse patients, these other judgment errors demonstrate a serious tearing of the fabric of the relationship. As you know, an employer has the right and responsibility to run its business as it sees fit. Balancing all the considerations, including your lack of judgment, trust, and respect, and your direct violation of known policies, it is in RISE UP's legitimate business interests to affirm the initial decision to terminate your employment. Your termination, for the reasons stated in Mr. Lowell's letter and in this one, stands.

Sincerely,

Ira Wrath

Ira Wrath, Esq.
Corporate General Counsel

cc: Sunol Day, President, RISE UP Intl.
      Steve Lowell, CEO, Manchester

Harold Starr, M.D.
123 Fourth St.
Manchester, NH 03105

October 13, 20XX

Ann Freed, Esq.
White Park Legal Services
Pond Way
Concord, NH 03301

Dear Alex:

Thank you for meeting with me on Tuesday. Attached is the summary of the events leading to my termination.

As you can imagine, this is a very difficult time for me. I was making about $110,000 per year, and suddenly I have no income. My youngest son is a college freshman, and because of my income we didn't qualify for any student loans. My oldest son just started law school, and I am helping him with his rent. I can't tell you how humiliating it was to be fired so publicly, but what is worse is having to tell my sons I can't support their dreams. In this small community, it will be tough to find a comparable job, given what happened. I did hear back from the prosecutor and they are going to drop my DWI charge. Consequently, I really need your help.

I understand that your associate will research whether I have a case. Please send me a copy of that memo because I need to understand the law as best I can. I trust that if there is no claim, you will level with me. Obviously, I am anxious to hear from you as soon as possible. I value your professional guidance, and I thank you for your help.

Sincerely,

Harold Starr, M.D.

Enc.

Summary of events leading up to my dismissal

Steve Lowell, the CEO at the Manchester clinic, and I have been good friends since he hired me as Medical Director over 20 years ago. We have worked together for the last 29 years. We frequently played golf at the country club and drank beers afterward. Occasionally we took our wives to dinner. At work, he took care of the corporate side of running the clinic, and I took care of the medical side. Steve has never given me a bad performance evaluation or issued any disciplinary action against me. No other employee has complained about my conduct, and in fact, I have been fortunate that management, staff, and patients have held me in high professional esteem.

On July 29, 20XX, I met with Conrad Howard, the father of one of my teenage patients, about his son's progress in managing chronic depression. At the end of the consult, Mr. Howard asked me a question about a recent bill for services. The itemized breakdown contained an obvious duplicate entry, a mistake that I said I would immediately correct. I kept the bill so we could document the error and send a corrected statement.

That evening, when I was finishing some paperwork at the office, I examined the bill more closely and was surprised to see that the hourly rate charged to Mr. Howard was twice the standard rate set by the RISE UP national headquarters in its rate schedule. The company advertises that nobody pays more than the low-est reimbursement rate they get from their lowest paying insurer. (See attached brochure.) I thought this doubled rate must be another mistake, but I had no way to confirm this because Steve, who takes care of the finances, was on a two-week vacation in Europe.

The RISE UP policy is that "technically," only the CEO is supposed to have access to the patient's personal financial information and contract for services. I say "tech-nically" because Steve frequently had me get financial information for him when he was out of the office. The information was all on his computer. He would call in and ask me to find a fee agreement and check on a date, or tell him whether he entered an agreement in the system yet. I'd use his password, find the docu-ment, and get him the information. This probably happened about once a month. There was never any issue between him and me about my accessing the financial records. I just never had any reason to actually read them before.

Over the next several days, I tried to obtain Mr. Howard's billing information from the billing center in Indiana, but my calls were routed through an automated system, and nobody responded to my messages. I wanted to respond to Mr. Howard promptly, and I didn't think Steve would mind if I took a look at the local documents, given our past pattern.

On August 5, when I still hadn't heard back from headquarters, I typed in Steve's password, clicked on "Contracts" and found Mr. Howard's folder. The first document was an online form. It contained Mr. Howard's home (billing) address, his residential property value from the City of Manchester property tax assessment card, and the value of a second home in Mr. Howard's name on Nantucket. It also listed his job as Senior Manager for a well-known investment firm, and his wife's job as a regional Vice President of Marketing for a large department store chain. They owned a Lexus SC10 and an Eddie Bauer Ford Explorer and had no other children. Insurance did not cover the clinic services. What was strange was that a name appeared on this form without any other explanation. The name was Bobby Banks. I recognized it because Bobby was one of the teenagers I had been treating on a pro bono basis.

Next, I clicked on a second document bearing Mr. Howard's name. It was a contract for services in which Mr. Howard agreed to pay an amount that was roughly double the national standard billing rate for as long as his son needed care. This seemed really odd to me because the company makes a big deal about only charging at the lowest insurance rate. Nor was there any reference in the contract that Mr. Howard was paying for any other patient's care or had agreed to do so. I thought that if Mr. Howard was making a charitable contribution, it would be mentioned somewhere in the file, especially for tax purposes, but it was not.

Next, I clicked on the file marked "Banks," thinking there might be some explanation there. In the spaces for the parents' address and occupation were the words, "Fees absorbed by Howard rate." There was no written contract or other financial information at all in the Banks online folder. I got really concerned. RISE UP makes a big deal in its national advertising about how it offers pro bono care to fully half the people it treats at every clinic. This is their way of "giving back" to the local community, but it is also a clever marketing strategy.

Over the next few days, I continued to review Steve's online files and discovered that for almost every patient who lived in the well-to-do sections of Manchester, the standard billing rate was doubled or even tripled, and there was always a pairing of a "fortunate" patient with one or sometimes two "pro bono" patients. I found 86 pairings.

I was shocked by this documentation because it contradicted the stated corporate policy about minimum fees. Moreover, the documents confirmed that it was not RISE UP that was providing the clinic's highly-touted pro bono services. (See brochure.) Rather the unknowing parents in the community were paying for the services, but RISE UP was taking the credit. Given the representations in the brochure, this seemed to me like fraud or at least some kind of intentional misrepresentation. I created a list of patients whose billing rates were inflated along with the pro bono clients with whom they were paired.

By the time Steve returned from his vacation on August 8, I had completed my list, but I was uncomfortable about confronting Steve because of our friendship. However, as a matter of professional integrity, I simply could not ignore what I had discovered. That day, I called the RISE UP Employee Hotline, in Indiana. It was established so that employees could make complaints just like this one, and they promised to handle them confidentially. The automated system instructed me to leave a name and number, and a human resources representative would call back. Later that day, an HR rep called back, and I reported my discovery to her. She asked for the list, which I e-mailed to her. She assured me that they would treat it all confidentially.

The next day, I was a wreck, so I took a vacation day on August 9. Since my wife, Margaret, was out of town, I headed to a bar that evening where I had a few drinks. Unfortunately, later that night, I was arrested for the DWI. I blew a .05, which I know is well below the legal limit. I have no prior driving record. After the police processed me, they let me make a phone call to a friend to pick me up at the station. I called Steve.

Steve's demeanor on the drive home was uncharacteristically icy, which I interpreted as Steve being upset that I bothered him in the middle of the night. In my driveway, I thanked him for the ride and friendship, and as I was closing the door, he suddenly yelled at me, "You stupid fool! Don't you get it? I make them money! You ruined everything just because you poked your self-righteous nose where it didn't belong! Get out, and I never want to see you again, you idiot." He sped away. I was stunned and confused. Although the Hotline call was supposed to be confidential, it was clear that someone had already talked to Steve.

The next morning, I went from home directly to the hospital to visit one of my patients. Then I headed to work for our weekly regional videoconference call. It involves all of the medical staff at approximately 15 New England clinics—about 150 people. When I walked into the videoconference room, the call was already going on. As soon as I sat down, Steve interrupted the speaker, and in front of nine members of my Manchester staff and everyone else on the call, he told me that I had to leave immediately because I was fired. Then, Steve told the security manager, who was waiting right there in the room, to immediately get my keys, laptop, Blackberry, and passwords, and to escort me through the waiting room and out the front door. Steve handed me a box containing some personal items he had already taken out of my office. The security guard escorted me through the staff work area and patient waiting room and out the front door. I have never been so humiliated in my life.

Steve refused to take my calls, and when I called the Hotline and left a message, nobody returned my call. From the August 10 to August 26, nobody gave me any reason for the termination. Finally, on August 26, I received the attached termination letter by registered mail. I really don't know what to do and look forward to receiving your advice as soon as possible.

RISE UP, Inc.
MEDICAL CLINICS

RISE UP, Inc. is a national chain of outpatient medical clinics that delivers high-quality medical and emotional health care to a frequently overlooked population, young adults (ages 15-21). These services include:

Drug and alcohol counseling
Mood disorder management
Family and relationship counseling
Sex education
Planned parenting counseling
Eating disorder management
Life coaching
And other services available on request

RISE UP, Inc. employs only the most qualified care providers from your local community.

Manchester, N.H.–based CEO, Steve Lowell, holds a Masters Degree in Health Administration and an MBA from Boston College. He has administered the Manchester facility since 1980, is nationally known for his work with adolescents, and has successfully raised three children of his own. He understands your personal and financial needs.

Manchester, N.H.–based Medical Director, Harold Starr, M.D. (Dartmouth Medical School, '71), maintained a successful private family practice in Londonderry, NH, for ten years before joining RISE UP. He has served as President of the Manchester Family Practitioners Council, as the family practice representative on the N.H. State Board of Medicine since 2008, and as a faculty member at Dartmouth Medical School.

THE RISE-UP PLEDGE

"RISE-UP" is an acronym for the corporate values of respect, integrity, service, and economy.

Respect. We pledge to conduct our relationship with you and your family with utmost respect for your private medical and financial information. All billing occurs at our national billing center in Indiana. The only transaction you will complete at the local level is to sign the initial service contract with the CEO.

Integrity. We pledge that our care providers shall maintain professional and private lives that model the physical and emotional health we advocate. Each employee remains substance and addiction free at all times.

Service. We pledge to serve you and your community. For every paying patient, the clinic will treat one pro bono patient from your community.

Economy. We pledge to provide services at the most economical rate possible. If you do not have insurance to cover our fees, you will only pay the same rate we receive from our lowest-paying insurer. We can do this because, as a national organization, we can take advantage of economies of scale. We will negotiate your fee for services individually with you.

UP is the direction your life will take when you work closely with us to improve your life or that of a loved one.

CHAPTER 15

Applying the Skills You Have Learned

Case file 3 gives you an opportunity to practice the skills you have learned. You will likely need to go back and review some of the sections in previous chapters. This book is written as a reference for you to use in law school and after you become a practicing lawyer. What follows is the approach you should take as you tackle case file 3.

A. GATHERING THE FACTS

As you did with case file 2, in the Starr case you need to carefully read through the documents and take notes on the facts. The information in the memorandum, the complaint, and the letter is what you have at this point, and you should base your research and analysis on the facts therein. You will notice that the parties do not look like they agree on all the facts. You should make this clear to your reader in your fact section and you will need to account for these differences in your analysis of the problem.

How do you write about facts that conflict? The best way to address conflicting facts is to alert the reader explicitly in the fact section that there are discrepancies. You do not need to mention the discrepancy in the issue or summary sections unless the discrepancy is the actual issue in the case or the discrepancy directly affects the analysis.

In case file 2, assume that one of the attendees of the study group claimed that she saw a large, stand-up, portable sign in May's apartment. The sign appeared to be the type of advertisement that would go on a sidewalk to advertise a business inside. This would conflict with other evidence in the file that May did not normally sell her jewelry from her apartment. In your fact section you would show this to the reader explicitly:

> May states that she only occasionally sells jewelry from her apartment. One of the attendees at the study group claimed she saw in May's apartment a portable sidewalk sign advertising her business. There is no evidence available to show how often or when May used the sign.

Notice that no attempt is made to justify, characterize, or explain the difference. You would only include a justification if it came from one of the parties in the case.

In your legal analysis, you may have to address how the conflicting facts could change the outcome of the case. For example, if in the May case there was the discrepancy about the whether she sold jewelry from her apartment more than just occasionally, you would have to show the reader that this information could change the outcome. For example:

> The presence in May's apartment of the portable advertising sign could provide evidence that would lead a court to consider her apartment as more of a business than a residence. Such a finding would support Hunt's invitee status. However, without more, the mere presence of the sign likely does not convert May's apartment to a business—particularly given that May does sell her jewelry at craft fairs and the sign may be used at these events,

This section would be part of your application. Where appropriate, you would show how the law might support an alternative interpretation, and then show how you would refute the interpretation.

B. USING THE FACTS TO GENERATE SEARCH TERMS FOR RESEARCH

Because you will be doing your own research, the way to get started in case file 3 is to use the facts to make a list of words you can use to find cases on point in New Hampshire. If you were conducting your own research in the May case, the list might look like this:

- Premises liability
- Business owner's liability
- Invitee
- Licensee
- Customer injury

If you use these words to do an electronic search, the words will get you to some of the relevant cases. From there you can begin reading cases and selecting the ones that look helpful. You can also use these words to find secondary sources. This is especially true for legal terms such as "premises liability."

PRACTICAL TIP

Many states have "Practice Series." These are volumes written by attorneys who specialize in an area of law. For example, there is usually a Family Law Practice Series or a Criminal Law Practice Series. Many of these can be found on Westlaw or LexisNexis or are available in hard copy in a law library. These volumes are a good place to get the lay of the land concerning the area of law you are researching in your jurisdiction. You may also want to consult other secondary sources to get a general idea about the legal issue you are researching.

CASE FILE 3: On Your Own—Review the Documents in Case File 3 and Make Notes

After reviewing and taking notes, make a list of words that you can use to generate research queries.

C. ORGANIZING CASES AND IDENTIFYING WHICH CASES TO USE

Your research for case file 3 will lead you to a number of cases and your task will be to narrow them down to the few that you'll need to answer the legal question. Remember to read and brief the cases that seem helpful. Study them and look for similar and distinguishable facts and rules that address wrongful termination. Once you have identified the cases that will guide your analysis of the problem, make an organizing chart like the one in Chapter 6. There may only be a few cases to use, but make sure any case you use is still good law and hasn't been overturned or narrowed.

D. START WRITING THE DISCUSSION SECTION

Remember the steps you go through in drafting the discussion from Chapter 8, which are repeated below. In case file 3, the legal issue has been identified for you, so you'll start with step 2.

1. Identify the legal issue.
2. Research the law.
3. Study the law.
4. Organize the information you have read.
5. Synthesize the rule(s).
6. Make an outline of your legal analysis.
7. Write a draft of the analysis.
8. Revise the draft.
9. Revise the draft again as needed.
10. Proofread and line edit.

Once you have researched and gathered the cases you think will be helpful, organize them using a chart or some other method that is suitable to your personal style. Students often ask how to know whether they have found enough cases. One way to feel reassured that your research is complete is if the opinions keep circling back to the same core cases when they cite to the rules. Shepardizing and Keyciting carefully will also help you know that you have read all the relevant cases. Remember, this process takes quite a bit of time, especially when you are first starting out as a lawyer.

CASE FILE 3: Assignment—Write the Rule on Wrongful Termination That Pertains to Your Case

After you write a draft of the rule, you are ready to draft the main roadmap paragraph and an outline. You may discover holes or questions about your analysis as you draft these. The research and case-studying process is ongoing during a project. Sometimes your analysis becomes clearer as you begin to draft and you need to re-read cases. That is a good thing! It shows that you are involved in an ever-recursive process of finding the best answer supported by the law—all signs of careful lawyering.

From your outline, write your first draft of the memorandum's discussion section. Keep in mind that this is likely to be revised substantially, but you need to get pen to paper to get the process going. Remember to consider and address the counter-analysis.

E. WRITING A NORMATIVE OR POLICY ANALYSIS

Very often there will be a piece of your legal discussion that calls for an analysis based on reason, policy, or normative societal standards. For example, negligence standards in tort law usually turn on issues of what is reasonable under the circumstances. To identify what is reasonable, courts often look to what the current norms are. When courts are resolving issues regarding new law or deciding a case where there is a split in court decisions, they frequently include some analysis that is based on norms to show why one result makes more sense than another. The *Diaz* case in Chapter 4 is an example of this type of reasoning.

Let's say, for example, that your supervisor tells you she has a client who was arrested for shoplifting. After the arrest, the police took her cell phone, opened it, and searched it. They found photos that incriminated the client. Your supervisor wants to know if the police searched the phone illegally. In your research you discover that the courts in your state have not definitively ruled on the issue. The decisions that come close to addressing it typically apply an analysis of traditional Fourth Amendment search and seizure law, but the courts also discuss the difficulty of applying Fourth Amendment law in the age of smartphones and laptops.

In writing the memorandum to your supervisor, in addition to explaining and applying the Fourth Amendment law, you will need to explain that the courts also consider current norms regarding new technology and phones. How do you do that? Unlike analogical reasoning based on precedent, normative reasoning has more of a narrative style. Here is an example of what you might say in a paragraph that would come after your application of the law:

> The defendant may be able to argue here that there is a meaningful difference between searching her iPhone and searching a wallet or purse. Although the court is likely to apply a traditional Fourth Amendment analysis, it is also likely that the court will recognize that new technologies allow for large amounts of private data to be stored on an iPhone. [Here you might cite to one of the cases that come close to your issue and use the normative analysis.] The type of information that can be stored of most relevance to law enforcement would be photographs, documents, e-mails, and written messages. With respect to those types of files, the only difference between the iPhone searched here and a laptop computer is the sheer volume of such materials that may be stored on each. If the state argues that the iPhone at issue here is merely a closed container, then warrantless laptop computer searches would also be permissible, a result that our court would probably think too far reaching.

Using a normative approach to answer a legal issue allows you to use your common sense. Though you must have a legal basis for using this type of analysis, the basis usually comes from cases where the court applied a normative analysis. Judges are people and they make decisions based on several things, including what makes sense. Courts are interested in keeping up with the times and refraining from illogical decisions. They are also interested in being fair and just. It will rarely be the case that you rely solely on a normative analysis. Usually, this piece of the analysis will be one paragraph or short section of an analysis that is otherwise based on cases and statutes.

F. REVISIONS

The first draft is just that; the final product may look very different. The revision stage may take almost as long as it took to research and write the first draft. Once you have a solid draft, consider using a checklist to help you edit further. Here is one example of a checklist, but you may also develop your own.

Issue
☐ Include decisive facts and legal question.

Summary (or Brief Answer)

- [ ] Start with a quick answer.
- [ ] Give the overall rule and apply it to the client's problem.
- [ ] Do not include legal citations.
- [ ] Limit to one paragraph.

Facts

- [ ] Include facts for context.
- [ ] Use an objective tone.
- [ ] Include decisive facts.
- [ ] Include all facts in the discussion section of the memorandum.
- [ ] Include both adverse and helpful facts for your client.
- [ ] Do not include legal citations.
- [ ] Include procedural history of client's case, if relevant.
- [ ] Tell a story that is logical and makes sense.

Main Roadmap Paragraph (NOTE: Your analysis may contain sub-rules that necessitate including mini-roadmaps.)

- [ ] In the first sentence, give the conclusion on the issue that applies the rule to the facts.
- [ ] State the overall statute/rule/test(s).
- [ ] Alert the reader to any givens or issues you are not going to address.
- [ ] Include policy *if* it is relevant to the overall rule.

Explanation of the Law

- [ ] Each paragraph should begin with a specific focus sentence or two that identifies the legal principle being discussed in the paragraphs.
- [ ] Organize the paragraphs around principles from the rule using topic or thesis sentences (and words) that alert the reader to which part of the rule you are explaining.
- [ ] Give brief examples from cases, if appropriate.

Application of the Law to Client's Problem

- [ ] Begin with a conclusion sentence that tells the reader where you are going.
- [ ] Show the reader how the rules apply to your client's facts using similar language to that used in the explanation of the law.
- [ ] Apply the rules or reasoning of the precedent to illustrate why your analogies or distinctions are significant and why the court will likely rule in line with your argument.
- [ ] Use clear sentence structure, concrete nouns and verbs, and transitions to communicate precisely and efficiently.
- [ ] The comparisons should be obvious and significant.
- [ ] The comparisons should refer to (not restate) decisive facts.

☐ The comparisons should include reasoning (why the comparison matters).

☐ Follow the same organization as in the explanation paragraphs.

Counter-Analysis

☐ Use words or phrases that alert the reader you are shifting to the counter-analysis.

☐ Give the specific alternative analysis.

☐ Show how the law might support the alternative analysis.

☐ Refute the counter-analysis.

Appendix

MEMORANDUM

To: Prof. Amy Vorenberg
From: Daniel Nathan
Date: November 8, 20XX
Re: Molly Jackson Negligence Action

Issue

Under Texas law, which holds a minor to a lesser standard of care than an adult, was Molly Jackson, a 14-year-old with intellectual disabilities, contributorily negligent when she was struck by Susan Green's car as she walked to her school bus stop wearing dark clothing and without a light?

Summary

Probably not. Texas courts measure a minor's standard of care by comparing it to the care that a child of the same age, intelligence, experience, and capacity would use. For a court to hold Molly contributorily negligent, it would have to find that she failed to meet this standard of care. Because of her mental challenges, a court would evaluate Molly by the standard of an ordinary ten year old and determine that a child of this age could not have foreseen the danger posed by the weather and road conditions. Thus, the court would likely find that Molly's failure to wear bright clothing or carry a light was reasonable and not contributorily negligent given her developmental age.

Facts

Our client, Molly Jackson, suffered serious injury after a car driven by Susan Green hit her as she walked to her bus stop. Molly is a 14-year-old girl who is intellectually and behaviorally four years behind others her age. Molly wants to sue Green for negligence. We must determine if Green is likely to succeed with an affirmative defense of contributory negligence.

Molly lives with her family near the bottom of Wagon Hill Road in Brownville. Molly's morning trip to the school bus had followed the same route every day for the prior three years. Molly would walk down her driveway and turn right. She would stay on the right-hand side of the road until she got to the top of the hill. At the top, she would check for traffic in both directions, cross to the left side of the street, and walk the rest of the way to her bus stop.

Last December 6, just after her 14th birthday, Molly left the house to go to the school bus as usual. She had not quite gotten to the top of the hill when Green's car hit her. It was early morning, dark, and the road was snow covered with snow banks along the shoulders. There were no sidewalks. Molly was wearing dark clothing and was not carrying a light.

Green was driving in the same direction on Wagon Hill Road at a modest speed. As another vehicle approached, Green dimmed her headlights. When she re-engaged her bright lights, she saw Molly in the road. Green hit Molly, causing her to suffer numerous internal injuries and several broken bones.

Discussion

A judge would probably not find Molly contributorily negligent because she acted with due care under the minor standard. A child between ages 5 and 14 may be contributorily negligent if the child failed to use such care as an ordinarily prudent child of the same age, intelligence, experience, and capacity would have exercised under the same or similar circumstances. *Rudes v. Gottschalk*, 324 S.W.2d 201, 206 (Tex. 1959); *MacConnell v. Hill*, 569 S.W.2d 524, 527 (Tex. App. 1978); *City of Austin v. Hoffman*, 379 S.W.2d 103, 107 (Tex. App. 1964); *Dallas Ry. & Terminal Co. v. Rogers*, 218 S.W.2d 456, 458 (Tex. 1949). A child's developmental capacity is relevant in assessing the correct standard of care to apply. *Soledad v. Lara*, 762 S.W.2d 212, 214 (Tex. App. 1988). Texas courts are reluctant to hold children responsible even if they failed to keep a proper lookout or heed warnings. *MacConnell*, 569 S.W.2d at 527. The test of negligence is different for children than for adults because the powers and abilities of children to anticipate danger and harmful consequences are often not the same as adults. *Rudes*, 324 S.W.2d at 206.

The standard of care applied to a child is measured by the behavior that would be reasonable under the circumstances given the child's particular abilities. *Houston & T.C.R. Co. v. Bulger*, 80 S.W. 557, 561 (Tex. App. 1904); *Soledad v. Lara*, 762 S.W.2d 212, 214 (Tex. App. 1988). In *Bulger*, a 13-year-old boy with an intellectual disability scalded both legs when hot water and steam escaped from a boiler at a railroad company's pumping station. 80 S.W. at 561. The court upheld the lower court's jury charge to consider the boy's low mental capacity, holding that the boy may not have had the same discretion that could reasonably be expected from other 13-year-old children. *Id*. Similarly, in *Soledad*, a 16-year old boy sued the design engineers of a drainage ditch where he was injured while playing. 762 S.W.2d at 214. The boy sued under the attractive nuisance doctrine and the court held that even though ordinarily the attractive nuisance doctrine does not apply to children over 14, it did apply in Soledad's case because the boy was lacking in mental development, as evidenced by his attendance in special education classes. *Id*.

Texas courts are reluctant to find children contributorily negligent where they have failed to keep a proper lookout for their own safety or to heed warnings. *See Guzman v. Guajardo*, 761 S.W.2d 506, 510 (Tex. App. 1988); *MacConnell*, 569 S.W.2d at 527. In *Guzman*, a seven-year-old boy was hit and killed by a car as he crossed a road. 761 S.W.2d at 510. The court upheld the lower court's decision that the boy was not contributorily negligent even though he was warned by his mother and grandmother specifically to stay off that particular road earlier that day. Id. Similarly, in *MacConnell*, a six-year-old boy was sprayed with hot steam and water when the defendant negligently removed the end of a car's radiator hose without first properly releasing the pressure. 569 S.W.2d at 525. The defendant had warned the boy twice to move away from the car. *Id*. The court reversed the lower court's jury decision that found the boy contributorily negligent, noting that the boy's failure to keep a proper lookout was not enough to bar his recovery because of his inferior ability to foresee and anticipate danger. *Id* at 528.

The experience and education of a child in the injury-causing activity does not necessarily make a child contributorily negligent. *Dallas Ry. & Terminal Co.*, 218 S.W.2d at 461; Guzman, 761 S.W.2d at 510. In *Dallas Ry. & Terminal Co.*, an 11-year-old girl familiar with the traffic hazards of downtown Dallas was hit by a bus as she crossed an intersection. 218 S.W.2d at 461. Reversing the jury's findings that the girl was contributorily negligent for failing to keep a proper lookout, the court held that even if a child has been instructed and is experienced in traffic matters, a higher standard of care should not be applied because the child is still subject to the reckless and impulsive nature of youth. *Id*. Similarly, the boy in Guzman was educated by his mother in traffic matters and was taught the importance of keeping a lookout for cars. *Guzman*, 761 S.W.2d at 510. The boy's traffic education did not affect the court's decision against finding him contributorily negligent. *Id*.

In evaluating Molly's potential contributory negligence, a court would first look at her age and mental capacity. Like the minors in *Bulger* and *Soledad*, who both showed signs of mental challenges, here testing has revealed that Molly is mentally and behaviorally four years behind other children her age. Although Molly was 14 years old at the time of the accident, the court will likely apply the standard of care of a ten-year-old child. Moreover, as in *Bulger*, where the court instructed the jury to consider that the child may not have had the same discretion that could be reasonably expected from other children of the same age, here the court is likely to give a jury the same instruction regarding Molly's developmental age.

A court would also probably determine that Molly, at her age and mental capacity, could not have foreseen the danger surrounding the circumstances on the day of the accident. Unlike *Guzman*, where the child's mother had instructed him in traffic safety, our facts do not indicate that Molly was warned about the hazards of walking to the bus stop on a dark, snowy street. Even if Molly had been warned of the danger on her road, it is unlikely that this would affect the court's decision in her favor given that in *Guzman* the warnings made no difference to the standard of care.

A court may determine that Molly's neglect to wear reflective clothing and to carry a light was a failure to keep a proper lookout for her safety. However, like the boy in *MacConnell*, Molly's inferior ability to anticipate danger as a minor should protect her from being held contributorily negligent. Her case may even be stronger than *MacConnell* because, arguably, she kept a proper lookout by walking on the right side of the street to the top of the hill until she could safely cross, thus avoiding the problem of non-visible oncoming traffic.

Molly's experience walking the same route for three years does not make it more likely that a court will find her contributorily negligent. Like the girl in *Dallas Ry. & Terminal Co.*, Molly was experienced in the everyday hazards presented by her route. Her manner of walking to the top of the hill before crossing the street is evidence that she was aware of traffic dangers. However, the girl's experience with traffic in *Dallas Ry. & Terminal Co.* did not make her contributorily negligent because her relative youth still could have lowered her ability to judge the circumstances. Similarly, Molly's experience with traffic should not increase the chance that a court will find her contributorily negligent.

Conclusion

A court will probably take into consideration Molly's ten-year-old mental capacity. Any evidence of Molly's experience in traffic matters, or her failure to keep a proper lookout or to heed warnings, is unlikely to result in a finding that permits Green to raise the affirmative defense of contributory negligence.

MEMORANDUM

To: Prof. Amy Vorenberg
From: Gabriel James
Date: November 17, 20XX
Re: Mary Kaufman (File #10002); Enforceability of Post-Employment
        Non-Competition Clause

Issue

Does Nebraska law permit enforceability of an employment agreement if it contains a non-compete clause restricting Livingston from seeking or gaining employment in any kitchen design firm or kitchen design related business within 50 miles of our client, Kaufman's place of business for a period of three years after cessation of employment.

Summary

The employment agreement is likely not enforceable. In Nebraska, covenant-not-to-compete clauses are enforceable only if they protect an employer's legitimate business interest, are not unduly harsh or oppressive on the employee, and are not injurious to the public. If a former employee has the opportunity to appropriate the goodwill of an employer's clients, the employer has a legitimate business interest in protecting that goodwill from unfair competition through the use of a post-employment covenant. The scope of protection must not be broader than reasonably necessary and cannot shield an employer from ordinary competition by a former employee. Additionally, the court applies a balancing test weighing the covenant's harshness upon the employee versus the benefit of the protection to the employer. Finally, the restrictions must not be detrimental to the public.

Kaufman can probably establish that there is a legitimate business interest in protecting the goodwill of her clients from unfair competition by Livingston because of the close working relationships he had with them. The covenant will probably not impose an undue hardship on Livingston because of his demonstrated talent outside of kitchen design and it will also probably not be injurious to the public because the market for kitchen design services is relatively small. However, the scope of the restriction is probably greater than reasonably necessary to protect the goodwill because it effectively prohibits ordinary competition with Kaufman, and therefore is unenforceable.

Facts

Our client, Kaufman Design Inc. is an Omaha, Nebraska design firm with a reputation for elegant kitchen designs that use regional natural materials. Livingston is a designer who established his reputation as an innovative home designer who specialized in the use of recycled products. Livingston signed a restrictive employment agreement with Kaufman, the enforceability of which has been called into question.

For a number of years prior to joining Kaufman, Livingston's work was featured in the media and through short articles he wrote on the use of recycled materials, and he was credited alone with developing sophisticated and innovative ways to use recycled materials. His work attracted many affluent clients through word of mouth and newspaper publicity.

In 2012, Livingston decided to specialize in kitchen design due to the lucrative nature of the work. He sought employment at a small design firm where he would have more opportunities to collaborate with other designers and gain expertise in kitchen design. Eventually Livingston signed a contract with Kaufman to work as a designer at her firm in Omaha. The contract included a post-employment covenant-not-to-compete. The restriction prevented Livingston from seeking or obtaining employment with any kitchen design firm or kitchen design related business within 50 miles of Omaha for three years after termination of employment.

Kaufman heavily promoted its relationship with Livingston and his expertise in innovative designs using recycled materials, and over a period of three years they collaborated on a number of kitchen design projects. One successful project was a kitchen designed for a high-profile client, and the resulting publicity generated many new clients for the firm. In 2015, Livingston abruptly resigned to study in Italy.

Recently Kaufman discovered from a contractor she regularly works with that Livingston had returned to Omaha and that one of her former clients had hired him to design a new kitchen using surface finishing techniques he had learned in Italy. The former client lives about 30 to 40 miles away from Kaufman's firm. Kaufman feels that Livingston may be violating the non-competition restriction and would like to see if it can be legally enforced.

Discussion

The covenant-not-to-compete clause of Livingston's employment agreement is probably not enforceable because it does not meet all three requirements for validity under Nebraska law. Nebraska law disfavors contracts in restraint of trade because they tend to stifle competition and are against public policy, and will only enforce such restraints if they are reasonable. *Mertz v. Pharmacists Mut. Ins. Co.*, 625 N.W.2d 197, 203 (Neb. 2001); *Philip G. Johnson & Co. v. Salmen*, 317 N.W.2d 900, 903-04 (Neb. 1982). A valid post-employment covenant not-to-compete requires that (1) the restriction must be reasonable in the sense that it is no greater than reasonably necessary to protect the employer in some legitimate interest, (2) the restriction must be reasonable in the sense that it is not unduly harsh and oppressive on the employee, and (3) the restriction must be reasonable in the sense that it is not injurious to the public. *Sec. Acceptance Corp. v. Brown*, 106 N.W.2d 456, 463 (Neb. 1960). The court has developed a balancing test to determine the reasonableness of such restrictive covenants. *Johnson*, 317 N.W.2d at 903-04. Reasonableness is determined on a case-by-case basis. *Am. Sec. Servs., Inc. v. Vodra*, 385 N.W.2d 73, 79 (Neb. 1986).

A. Legitimate Business Interest

Although Kaufman likely has a legitimate business interest, the court will probably find that the covenant not-to-compete is unenforceable because the restriction is greater than reasonably necessary to protect her company's goodwill. Post-employment restraints on competition by former employees may protect an employer's legitimate business interest from unfair competition, but restrictions on ordinary competition are not valid or enforceable. *Polly v. Ray D. Hilderman & Co.*, 407 N.W.2d 751, 755 (Neb. 1987) (quoting *Vodra*, 385 N.W.2d at 78); *Boisen v. Petersen Flying Serv., Inc.*, 383 N.W.2d 29, 33 (Neb. 1986). Unfair competition is distinguished from ordinary competition by evaluating an employee's opportunity to appropriate goodwill from the employer. *Boisen*, 383 N.W.2d at 33. Competitive use of information or relationships acquired in the course of an employee's employment with an employer is considered unfair and the employer is legitimately entitled to protection from it. *Id*. at 34.

Where an employee has the opportunity to siphon customer goodwill away from the employer, the employer can use a post-employment covenant not-to-compete to protect that goodwill. *Boisen*, 383 N.W.2d at 33; *Polly*, 407 N.W.2d at 755. For example, in *Polly*, where an accountant had substantial personal contact with approximately 46 of his employer's accounts, the court found that the accounting firm had a legitimate interest in protecting itself against the accountant's opportunity to appropriate customer goodwill—in the form of those customers after his employment was terminated. 407 N.W.2d at 755. On the other hand, in *Boisen*, the court reasoned that a flying service had no legitimate interest in shielding itself from ordinary competition with an aerial spraying pilot who had no personal or business contacts with any of the employer's customers and thus no opportunity to lead those customers away. 383 N.W.2d at 34-35.

However, even if an employer establishes that there is a legitimate business interest to protect, the covenant not-to-compete must not be greater than reasonably necessary to protect that interest. *Polly*, 407 N.W.2d at 755; *Moore v. Eggers Consulting Co.*, 562 N.W.2d 534, 540 (Neb. 1997). Generally, a covenant is valid only if it restricts the former employee from working for or soliciting the former employer's clients with whom the employee had personal contact. *Polly*, 407 N.W.2d at 756. Because the covenant in *Polly* attempted to restrict the accountant from soliciting clients he did not know, the court found that the restriction was greater than reasonably necessary to protect against unfair appropriation of client goodwill. *Id*. Likewise, in *Moore*, a covenant prohibiting a former employee from working as a recruiter anywhere in the continental United States was unenforceable because its scope was greater than reasonably necessary to prevent the recruiter from soliciting the employer's clients. 562 N.W.2d at 540.

Here, the court will probably find that Kaufman has a legitimate, protectable business interest. Kaufman described how Livingston worked closely with a high-profile client to design a kitchen, which subsequently created a lot of publicity for the firm and brought in many new clients. Although Livingston did not officially have any of his own clients at Kaufman, he had worked closely with a number of them. As in *Polly* and

Moore, where the employees had substantial personal contact with their employers' clients, Livingston likewise has an opportunity to appropriate Kaufman's client's goodwill through his relationships with them. Given his specialty in kitchen design, the goodwill of Kaufman's clients is legitimately entitled to protection from unfair competition by Livingston.

Nevertheless, even if Kaufman is entitled to protect her legitimate business interest, the scope of the restriction is probably greater than reasonably necessary because it is not limited to solicitation of clients with whom Livingston actually did business. The restriction is broader, prohibiting Livingston from seeking or obtaining employment in any kitchen design capacity within 50 miles of Omaha, regardless of whether such employment would constitute unfair competition by Livingston. As in *Moore*, where the covenant was broader than reasonably necessary because it failed to limit the scope of the recruiting restriction, and *Polly*, where the covenant attempted to prohibit the accountant from working for clients unknown to him, here Kaufman is attempting to prohibit Livingston from soliciting kitchen design services solely on the basis of a large geographical area without regard to the existence of relationships Livingston may have with those potential clients. Because the policy is to only shield an employer from unfair competition, such a broad unqualified restriction is probably greater than reasonably necessary to protect Kaufman from ordinary competition by Livingston.

B. Undue Employee Hardship

The protection of Kaufman's legitimate business interest probably outweighs any hardship of the covenant not-to-compete on Livingston when the balancing test is applied to the circumstances here. A covenant not-to-compete must not be unduly harsh or oppressive on the employee. *C & L Indus., Inc. v. Kiviranta*, 698 N.W.2d 240, 247 (Neb. Ct. App. 2005) (quoting *Brown*, 106 N.W.2d at 463); *see also Dow v. Gotch*, 201 N.W. 655, 656-57 (Neb. 1924) (finding no fraud or duress upon a hairdresser entering into restrictive contract). The court has adopted a "balancing test" to help determine if a covenant is unduly harsh or oppressive. *Johnson*, 317 N.W.2d at 904. Considerations and factors involved in this balancing test include "the degree of inequality in bargaining power; the risk of the covenantee losing customers; the extent of respective participation by the parties in securing and retaining customers; the good faith of the covenantee; the existence of sources or general knowledge pertaining to the identity of customers; the nature and extent of the business position held by the covenantor; the covenantor's training, health, education, and needs of his family; the current conditions of employment; the necessity of the covenantor changing his calling or residence; and the correspondence of the restraint with the need for protecting the legitimate interests of the covenantee." *Id.*

In applying the balancing test, the harshness and oppressiveness on the employee must be weighed against an employer's legitimate business interest in protecting goodwill. *Vodra*, 385 N.W.2d at 80; *Johnson*, 317 N.W.2d at 904. For example, in *Vodra*, the manager at a security company, who had acquired all of his security services skills on the job and was in good health, agreed to a narrowly drafted non-competition restriction which the court later concluded was not unduly harsh or oppressive in light of the employer's legitimate business interest in protecting its clients' goodwill. *Id.* Similarly, the court found in *C & L* that a post-employment covenant on a staffing supervisor was not unduly harsh and oppressive because the restriction still allowed her to solicit "thousands" of companies on behalf of her new employer and would not force her to give up a job with a competing company. 698 N.W.2d at 251. Additionally, because the supervisor had capitalized on the relationships with clients that she developed with her previous employer, the court, in balancing the relevant factors, held that the employer's interest in protecting its goodwill outweighed any hardship against the supervisor; thus, the covenant was reasonable and enforceable. *Id.*

Applying the balancing test here shows that the restrictions are probably not unduly harsh or oppressive on Livingston. Livingston developed skills in his trade both prior to and after working for Kaufman, and has demonstrated success in areas other than kitchen design. Although Livingston may feel that kitchen design is a more lucrative specialty than other areas in which he is skilled, he will probably not have difficulty maintaining his livelihood in other ways using the training he acquired in Italy. As in *Vodra*, where the non-compete covenant did not force the manager to relocate or totally restrict his activities within the region, here the covenant would not force Livingston to relocate if he chooses to practice aspects of interior design other than kitchens.

On the other hand, it could be argued that, unlike *C & L*, where the supervisor was allowed to solicit "thousands" of companies not restricted by the covenant, here there is no evidence that Livingston has access to such a large base of potential clients. Indeed, his specialty is generally only sought after by affluent clients who are a relatively small segment of the population, and Kaufman admits that she will likely lose a lot of business to Livingston if he is allowed to practice kitchen design in the area. However, Livingston has already solicited one of Kaufman's former clients (possibly in bad faith), just as the staffing supervisor did in *C & L*, and when the balancing test is applied to these facts the considerations weigh more heavily in favor of protecting Kaufman's business interest than any potential hardship against Livingston.

C. Public Injury

Kaufman's post-employment covenant is probably not injurious to the public because the public would not appreciably be denied kitchen design services as a result of the restriction on Livingston. A covenant not-to-compete is against public policy if it has a "mischievous tendency, and in some way militates against the public welfare and the rights of the public." *Chambers-Dobson, Inc. v. Squier*, 472 N.W.2d 391, 400 (Neb. 1991); *Dow*, 201 N.W. at 657. In *Dow*, the court said that a city did not "suffer" from a post-employment restriction preventing a beautician from working there, for it had "beauty parlors a plenty." 201 N.W. at 657. Implying that the public would not be denied access to such services if the beautician were not allowed to work there, the court held that the employment contract was valid and enforceable. *Id*. Likewise, in *Chambers*, the court concluded that a covenant prohibiting an insurance agent from soliciting a fraction of the total population of region did not deny access of the agent's services to an appreciable number of the public and did not violate public policy. 472 N.W.2d at 400.

Livingston's post-employment restrictions are probably not injurious to the public. While there are not "kitchen designers a plenty" in Omaha—unlike in *Dow*, where there was no apparent shortage of parlors—reasonably there is not a large number of the public who would suffer if Livingston is prohibited from practicing kitchen design there, similar to the situation in *Chambers*, where very few potential clients were off-limits to the agent. Because the covenant would deny access to Livingston's kitchen design services to so few people, it is difficult to argue that the covenant is injurious to the public and against public policy.

Conclusion

Kaufman will probably not be able to enforce the non-compete clause against Livingston. Although Kaufman can show a legitimate business interest in protecting the goodwill of her clients, the restriction is overly broad in scope because it completely prohibits Livingston from competing in the regional kitchen design business. The harshness of the restriction upon Livingston does not outweigh the reasonableness of protecting Kaufman's business interest. Because the restriction on Livingston's ability to perform kitchen design would not detriment an appreciable number of people, the covenant cannot be considered injurious to the public welfare or the rights of the public.

Index